Participation and Mediation

Participation and Mediation

*A Practical Theology
for the Liquid Church*

Pete Ward

scm press

Scripture quotations are from the New Revised Standard
Version of the Bible, copyright 1989 by the Division of Christian
Education of the National Council of the Churches of Christ in
the USA. Used by permission. All rights reserved.

British Library Cataloguing in Publication data
A catalogue record for this book is available
from the British Library

978 0 334 04165 8

First published in 2008 by SCM Press
13–17 Long Lane,
London EC1A 9PN

www.scm-canterburypress.co.uk

SCM Press is a division of
SCM-Canterbury Press Ltd

Typeset by Regent Typesetting, London
Printed in the UK by CPI William Clowes
Beccles NR34 7TL

Contents

Acknowledgements

There are a number of people I want to thank because they helped me enormously as I was writing this book. First I am grateful to my colleagues Andrew Walker and Luke Bretherton, who, along with all the students in the Centre for Theology, Religion and Culture, have made King's College London such a vibrant and supportive place to work. I am particularly grateful to Clemens Sedmak, who has so kindly read and commented on my work.

I am also greatly indebted to Gordon Lynch, who has been a real source of encouragement at various stages in the project. Once or twice he helped me to see the wood for the trees, and his advice and comments have helped give a shape and coherence to the book, which might have eluded me without his guidance. I want to say thank you as well to Elaine Graham, who generously read sections of the text in the very early stages of development. Also to Martyn Percy, who gave me helpful feedback on an early draft of the manuscript. I want to thank Paul Fiddes for his kind support and comments on my work over the last three or four years. Some of the ideas that form the middle sections of this book had an early outing in a paper that Paul and I presented at Yale Divinity School in September 2007. I want also to thank John Swinton, Chris Scharen and Ryan Bolger for their enthusiasm for the project. It has made all the difference to be told from time to time that you might be on to something when you are buried in the middle of things. Finally and most importantly I want to thank Tess, Eleanor and Callum for putting up with a partially zombified and rather preoccupied husband and father over the last three years or so.

I have been grateful for the opportunity to test out my ideas by giving papers and public lectures. I am grateful in particular for invitations to speak at Fuller Seminary in Pasadena, the Henry Martyn Centre,

Cambridge, the Department of Theology and Religion, Durham, Ripon College, Cuddesdon and the Oxford Centre for Mission Studies. Some of the ideas that I developed in this book have been published in their early stages elsewhere. I wish to thank Bryan Spink for an invitation to speak at the Institute for Sacred Music in Yale. My address was published in the *Yale Institute for Sacred Music Colloquim: Music, Worship, Arts*.[1] An earlier version of Chapter 7 was published in Gordon Lynch's edited volume *Between Sacred and Profane*.[2]

Pete Ward
Oxford
April 2008

1 Ward, P. (2006), 'Mediating the Mediator: A Cultural Theology of Culture', in *Yale Institute for Sacred Music Colloquim: Music, Worship, Arts*, vol. 3, autumn.

2 Ward, P. (2007), 'The Eucharist and the Turn to Culture', in Lynch, G. (ed.), *Between Sacred and Profane: Researching Religion and Popular Culture*, London: I. B. Tauris.

Introduction

'So what was it that inspired you to write this book?' asks the day-time TV presenter. It's an invitation for the author to reflect on the origins of their writing. The question is a cliché, but also a classic. It is a classic because it makes the writer tell the audience how the ideas behind the book connect with their personal life. The question orientates the conversation towards the experiential. The reference to inspiration is particularly telling. Inspiration is a prompt to talk about the significance of these ideas and the difference they have made to the author's own life. The presenter wants the writer to bare something of his or her soul. So the question draws them into a conversation that touches upon the nature of their commitment to what they have written. Choosing this question as a starting point is not so much an attempt to give practical theology a daytime TV make-over (however tempting that may be) – rather, it comes from the recognition that there is something to learn from this small slice of popular culture. It is an indication of the way that ideas, and books that contain ideas, seem to be more accessible to us if we can find a way to connect them to the writer's experience of life.

The desire to connect ideas to the personal and social is not solely the preserve of popular television. Many of us, when we pick up a theo-logical book for the first time, start by reading the personal acknowl-edgements in the preface. My interest in these personal statements owes a great deal to my desire to give some kind of a context to the authors and their ideas. I want to know where they are coming from, and the acknowledgements give a brief but tantalizing hint about what inspired them to write. Reading between the lines of what a writer says in these opening pages can offer a good many clues to the cultur-ally curious reader. They may get a glimpse of the author's intellectual conversation partners, they may perhaps learn about his or her faith community, and occasionally catch a glimpse of family background. Reading acknowledgements in this way is a kind of 'textual poaching', to borrow a term from Michel de Certeau.[3] This way of approaching a theological text is poaching because it seeks to find a context in the social, the historical and the personal that the author may not have intended to provide. Of course not all theological texts require us to use our poacher skills to locate their ideas in a context. As well as the many explicitly 'contextual' theologies there is an increasing trend towards the desire to situate even the most abstract theological arguments within specific social and cultural settings.[4]

This book, like other theological works, has a particular setting and origin. It is a work of theory exploring the theological and cultural shape of practical theology. Yet this theoretical project has a context, a setting in life that came originally from my experience as a ministerial practitioner. A consideration of where the writer is 'coming from' has become a formal and structured part of many kinds of academic enquiry. This form of reflection is generally referred to as 'reflexivity'.[5] I want to adopt this method of reflexivity as an introduction to the theories that follow. There are two reasons for this. The first is that reflexivity helps to focus attention on the situatedness of theory. I first came to practical theology, and issues of spirituality and culture, through the challenges I encountered when I was working as a Christian youth worker. So I had my feet firmly planted in practice even if my head was often to be found buried in a book. In my academic life I continue to work with youth ministers and other ministerial practitioners and I have sought to develop theoretical perspectives, which help them, not simply to critically interact with their ministerial contexts but perhaps more importantly to generate theology which can energize and animate their own ministerial practice. This book is part

---

3 de Certeau, M. (1984), *The Practice of Everyday Life*, trans. Rendall, S., Berkeley: University of California Press, p. xii; see also Jenkins, H. (1992), *Textual Poachers: Television Fans and Participatory Culture*, London: Routledge.

4 A good example of this would be Volf, M. (1996), *Exclusion and Embrace*, Nashville: Abingdon Press.

5 Johnson, R., Chambers, D., Rahuram, P. and Tincknell, E. (2004), *The Practice of Cultural Studies*, London: Sage; see also Swinton, J. and Mowat, H. (2006), *Practical Theology and Qualitative Research*, London: SCM Press, p. 59.

of that project. The second reason for introducing this work through reflexivity relates to a central argument of the book, namely, that cultural studies offers 'a way of seeing' that can be a considerable help as we do practical theology. Adopting a reflexive method is a way of illustrating this point.

Reflexivity and Practical Theology

Reflexivity is an intentional and disciplined form of reflection on how the personal, social and cultural context of the researcher not only affects what is researched, that is, the choice of a particular field of study, but also the way that that research is conducted. It is a process of self-examination where the researcher attempts to disclose how personal, social and cultural factors have affected their work. This kind of reflection has emerged from a widespread acceptance of the extent to which academic reflection and analysis is itself, 'cultural through and through'.[6] What this means is that academic work is situated in a setting in life. Research comes from and in turn has an influence upon social, historical and personal contexts. John Swinton describes reflexivity as, 'a mode of knowing which accepts the impossibility of the researcher standing outside of the research field and seeks to incorporate that knowledge creatively and effectively'.[7]

Reflexivity is understood in a variety of ways. One version of reflexivity argues that self-understanding can lead to the correction of bias.[8] An alternative approach treats reflexivity as a way of informing readers of positions and partialities so that they are then able to make adjustments and judgements on what is being said.[8a] At its most basic, reflexivity relates to a process of disclosure and dialogue that is intended to make evident the situated and interested nature of academic work. It is this third, and more general, approach to reflexivity that I want to adopt. This kind of reflexivity is a strategic and crucial move in practical theology because it encourages methods of enquiry that value and have a place for commitment. Commitment would of course include faith and belief. So reflexivity then is a way of showing how a practical

---

6 Johnson et al., *Practice*, p. 44.

7 Swinton and Mowat, *Practical*, p. 59.

8 and 8a Johnson et al., *Practice*, p. 52.

theology grows out of a particular personal history, social context and theological tradition. Adopting reflexivity should not, then, be seen as an attempt to find some form of objectivity but rather it is an acknowledgement that the commitments of the writer are a part of the academic process. In fact they are a vital and creative aspect of any practical theology.

My approach to reflexivity is based around autobiography. It sets out to offer an account of the generation of theory from a rich mix of ministerial practice, spiritual experience and an exploration of the Christian tradition. My term for this form of reflexivity is 'auto/theobiography'. This practice of reflexivity is based on the assumption that accepting the cultural situatedness of knowing necessarily involves an acceptance of the practice of faith and personal believing as a part of that knowing. In fact I want to argue that these factors need to be discussed as a key starting point for theological reflection. Auto/theobiography combines autobiography with theology. This form of reflexivity is autobiographical because it is an intentional method designed to set out how my own experience first as a ministerial practitioner and then as an academic engaged in teaching practitioners gave rise to this particular theoretical enterprise, that is to say, the attempt to theorize practical theology as participation and as mediation. At the same time this form of reflexivity is theological because it is rooted first in my own theological commitment (to the Church, to a theological tradition, and to a sense of vocation in ministry) and second it has grown from my spiritual life as a worshipping, praying member of the Christian community. Auto/theobiography therefore situates practical theology as a theoretical practice in the theological and the cultural. This is the main reason why I have adopted this approach to reflexivity, because it is an attempt to guard against the counter-productive and counter-intuitive implications involved in developing a theory of the relationship between the study of culture and practical theology as if it were an entirely abstract or 'objective' enterprise, which it is not.

Youth Ministry and Commitment

Before I became a full-time academic I was a youth minister. Being a youth minister meant that for the first twenty years of my working life

I was employed in a variety of roles that were all focused on sharing the Christian faith with young people. Throughout this time I was particularly concerned to find ways to build missional relationships with young people who in the normal run of things would never darken the doors of the Church. Looking back it is clear to me that my work with young people grew out of a theological conviction. The conviction was based on a belief that God cared passionately for those who didn't come to church. I got involved in youth ministry because I felt a calling to find ways to express God's love for these young people who for one reason or another found themselves outside the Christian community.[9]

In Britain the majority of young people have little or no connection with church or church-based youth work. I recall being asked to preach in one of the college chapels in Oxford, where I live, about my vision for ministry with young people. I took as my text the parable of the shepherd and the lost sheep. In the parable the shepherd has 100 sheep but one of them has wandered off. So the shepherd leaves the remaining 99 to go in search of the one that has lost its way. I made the point that in the parable the 99 can be read as the faithful while the shepherd probably represents Jesus. The parable was an explanation of Jesus' ministry, which was primarily focused on those who were outside the fold. I saw youth ministry as a calling to follow this example. The crucial difference, I pointed out, was that in our contemporary context the numbers are reversed. A rough numerical estimate of the extent of the Church's youth work in the UK is probably that we have a meaningful contact with between 5 and 10 per cent of young people who are between the ages of 15 and 25. This means that the vast majority of Christian youth work is focused on what is actually a relatively small number of young people. To return to the parable, I argued that for all our efforts we did not have 99 but had one sheep in our fold and this single sheep is getting all of our attention. So we have a very pampered and well-groomed sheep attending our church meetings, and yet at the same time we seem to have very little concern for the 99 who are off doing their own thing. I saw youth ministry as a vocation or a specific

---

9 I have written about my experience as a youth minister elsewhere; see Ward, P. (1992), *Youth Culture and the Gospel*, London: Marshall Pickering; Ward, P. (1993), *Worship and Youth Culture*, London: Marshall Pickering; and Ward, P. (1997), *Youthwork and the Mission of God*, London: SPCK.

calling to find ways to redress this balance. Most ministers saw their role as looking after the sheepfold but I saw the task of ministry as a calling to search for those who were not being cared for. The key difference from the parable was that in the present-day scenario most of the sheep were out and about doing their own thing.

Looking back I realize that it was this calling to those outside the Christian community, and particularly to young people, that has shaped my theological journey more than anything else. As an academic working in a university setting this vocation still lies at the heart of my own sense of identity. I do what I do because of this calling, and my research interests have grown out of the various theological questions that have come from trying to do Christian youth work with those who are not part of the church 'in crowd'. In this sense I am a committed academic or an academic with commitments. I am an insider to the Christian community trying to make sense of my faith in relation to a particular ministerial practice. As an 'insider' I have been committed to ministerial practice among young people. In this work I am part of a community of practice and a theological tradition. For Etienne Wenger a community of practice involves participation in communal learning. 'Participation here refers not just to local events of engagement in certain activities with certain people, but to a more encompassing process of being active participants in the practices of social communities and constructing identities in relation to these communities.'[10] To be a participant in a group in the playground or a team in the workplace is both an action, says Wenger, and a belonging. Participation shapes our sense of ourselves and influences how we interact with those around us.[10a]

Christian youth work is just this kind of community of practice. It is made from the participation of young people and leaders in local churches, at Christian camps and house parties, and at summer events and festivals. During the last thirty years this community of practice has been expanded as churches in the UK have started to employ people as youth workers. The academic work that I am involved in at King's College London has emerged as a response to the growth in numbers of Christian youth workers seeking professional develop-

10 and 10a Wenger, E. (1998), *Communities of Practice: Learning, Meaning, and Identity*, Cambridge: Cambridge University Press, p. 4.

ment. So my practice of teaching forms a part of the flow of learning within this specific community of practice. I am therefore explicitly conscious that I write from within this community and my intention is to play a critical but also a creative and helpful part in the ongoing conversation in this community.

As well as being a part of the community of practice in the field of church-related youth work I am also a Christian. These two are not unrelated. My sense of self as a ministerial practitioner and now as a teacher is bound up with my spiritual experience. This is what I mean by using the phrase 'vocation' and calling. I was doing what I was doing as a youth minister because of a spiritual journey. Youth ministry as I experienced it was about sharing in God's concern for young people who were outside the life of the Church. My practice was not simply a job, it was a participation in a spiritual realm, a sharing in the divine mission, that is to say, God's love for young people outside of the Church. As I have moved from direct work with young people to the practice of research and teaching in a university I have continued to see my work as part of this calling. So practical theology forms part of my sense of call. It is spiritually and missionally orientated. I recognize that some people who do not share my commitments may want to engage in the critical reflection on the expression and practice of the Church, but this does not mean that they will be commitment-neutral, simply that they have different commitments. So I am not suggesting my take on practical theology is the right way, merely that it is right for me given my commitments, and to the extent that the reader may share those commitments it may also be right for them.

Ministry and Theology

As I have said, my interest in practical theology came directly from my experience working as a youth minister. From the start I was acutely aware that youth ministry, as I understood it, presented some testing and quite difficult challenges. Around the time that I began my work as a Christian youth worker I came across a book by John Bennington.[11]

---

11 Bennington, J. (1973), *Culture, Class and Christian Beliefs*, London: Scripture Union.

Bennington's work echoed my own experience of trying to be a youth minister with those who were at a distance from the Christian Church. In what is often an angry and despairing book he explores his own failure as a Christian youth worker.[12] *Culture, Class and Christian Beliefs* centres around an account of Bennington's attempt to do Christian youth work with a small group of working-class young people. Here, Bennington records three young people, Kes, Chris and Charlie, talking about the tensions they experienced between their new-found faith and their working-class background:

> Kes: I don't know, the cost isn't so much material things. It's pride and self assurance, you know what I mean ... People regarding you as soft and stupid ... I know a lot of my brother's mates, all blokes of about fourteen and fifteen and that, regard me as stupid. I mean the way they talk to me and the way they look at me, they just think I'm stupid
>
> Charlie: Well I mean ...
>
> Kes: No but I mean straight up! And that hurts because ... well it just does, you know. But it's pride. I mean as a Christian, you lose your identity, don't you?
>
> Chris: But you find a new one, don't you?
>
> Charlie: Do you, though?
>
> Kes: I don't know. I mean you might have a notoriety to do something: 'Go away! Him! You know Charlie: fifteen pints a night and still drive home sober!' That sort of stuff. But after you're a Christian, they say, 'Yeah, we used to see him down the pub now and again. Used to drink a bit' and in the end, 'Charlie? Oh Him! He's just a bible puncher.'[13]

Kes, Charlie and Chris appear to have been open to the Christian faith. They have started to identify themselves as Christian but there are problems. They are expressing their sense that through their Christian commitment they have somehow lost their identity. In their faith they have a new identity but they feel that they have become dislocated from

---

12 I should say at this point that I do not see any essential difference between the terms Christian youth worker and youth minister, and so I use the terms interchangeably.

13 Bennington, *Culture*, pp. 23–4.

their community and its social world. In the end the cultural and social demand of believing was to prove too costly and as the story unfolds, sadly these young people eventually choose to abandon their Christian commitment.

Culture, Class and Christian Belief was an uncomfortable book but it captured many of the issues I was facing as a Christian youth worker. Like Bennington I had found that the problem was not really the lack of a willingness or openness to faith on the part of the young people I knew. My experience was that, provided a youth minister was able to develop long-term, committed and honest relationships with young people, many of them were more than ready to consider faith as an option in their life. What they found more of a challenge was the wider Christian community and the institution of the Church. They were attracted to faith and spiritual experience but they found it almost impossible to identify with formal religious life. It was this problematic of young people coming to faith and yet rejecting the existing forms of church life that has driven my theological work, and it is this particular ministerial context that has shaped the argument of this book.

The assumption behind most Christian youth work is that young people, as they come to faith, will join the Church. Joining the Church means that they will take on the social and cultural norms of the community. These norms are not simply ethical or behavioural: they also encompass the way that faith is expressed in the Christian community. The point I am trying to make is that churches have a particular 'culture' that is evident in every aspect of their communal life. This includes styles of worship (in particular musical expression), ways of organizing, ways of socializing, styles of leadership, and so on. Being accepted as part of a local church requires a cultural competence in understanding and making use of the specific forms of expression used by the community. For those young people who have grown up in Christian families this competence has come as they have been brought to church as children by their parents. For those who join church at a later stage, participation in church life depends on the ability to develop the required competencies. Being a part of the Christian community means that a person shares in the culturally located expression of the Church. One way of understanding church-based youth work is that it has evolved as a way to address these cultural issues. Christian youth

9

work has traditionally been based around some kind of youth group. In the youth group the young people can find fellowship and learn the faith by sharing in the activities of the group. If an outsider chooses to join the group and they eventually come to faith they are in turn socialized into the cultural forms of expression of the Church. The youth group is a way of learning faith not simply as conviction and belief but also as a form of behaviour and expression, that is, a church culture.

My own approach to youth ministry was based on the realization that church youth groups were limited in their appeal. I had quickly found that there are ways to be 'successful' in reaching out to a broader range of young people than those usually attracted by church-based groups. At the same time I realized that my new approach to outreach effectively bypassed the usual processes of socialization and discipleship that operated in church youth work. Young people were coming to faith, but this only served to emphasize the cultural and theological problems in ministry when it is conducted beyond the certainties of church culture. At the time, my sense was that these young people were adopting faith but within a different cultural and social setting to the normal church group. This raised the question of the relationship between faith, its expression in culture, and the way that church communities develop and reproduce themselves through their particular culture. At the heart of these issues lay the question of the relationship between theology and culture. As I was turning these issues over in my mind I came across the field of mission studies.

Mission Studies

What I began to realize was that my work as a youth minister was fundamentally related to finding creative ways to do theology while simultaneously trying to negotiate a way to do this within the context of cultural difference. At a most basic level there was the challenge of finding how to express faith to and with young people in ways that connected with their lives. The problem was that faith as I understood it, and had learned it in my church community, was already expressed in culturally specific forms, such as in ways of worshipping, meeting together, praying, living, and so on. Like Bennington before me it was the young people that I knew who made me aware of the extent to which faith, as I had learned it, was a specific expression within culture. So by stepping outside of the church cultural bubble I had begun to relativize my own expression of faith.

The kind of work I was doing was not simply based on trying to overcome the fact that young people were outside of the Christian community or not attending its groups. What I also discovered was that they found the expression of faith within these groups to be inappropriate. As I started to look through their eyes and appreciate their perspective I became acutely aware of the extent to which the Christian community was socially and culturally dislocated from the world of these young people.

I began to see that the issues I was facing did not really come from the young people themselves. The problem was not really anything to do with 'youth culture' or the social world and norms of the young people. There was something which was much more fundamental and theological at stake in my ministerial practice. I was engaged in a theological task of translating faith from the culturally specific expression of my own church community into a new context. Yet just as this kind of ministry was involving me in the translation of faith as expression and practice, it also raised the question of how Church itself might be reshaped. In other words, what I realized was that my attempt at doing youth ministry seemed to share a good deal in common with mission studies in that its primary focus lay in the questions which surround the translation of faith from one cultural context to another and how this kind of expression would eventually shape the life of the Church. I was helped to make this connection between Christian youth work and mission studies through the writings of the missiologist Charles Kraft.

In *Christianity in Culture*, Kraft tells of his own experience as a missionary in Northern Nigeria.[14] He describes his confusion when he found that the theological formulations he had been taught as universal truth in his US seminary seemed to be misunderstood or to lack plausibility in the African context. Faced with cultural difference he began to recognize that his own understanding of faith was itself largely culturally conditioned, and if he was to ever find a way to share

---

14 Kraft, C. H. (1979), *Christianity in Culture*, Maryknoll: Orbis.

this faith in a new culture he would have to find ways to translate his theology from one cultural context to another.[15] Drawing on his anthropological training, Kraft was able to interpret his confusion as having its roots in cultural differences. Yet these cultural differences were actually presenting as theological problems. His theological training had taught him to keep his theology and his anthropology separate. What he realized, however, was that the question of translation demanded that he work with these two disciplines at the same time.[16] At one point Kraft describes how one of his missionary colleagues was attempting to combine anthropology with theology. His approach involved an in-depth study of the Nigerian culture. Having developed a cultural analysis of the people he was working with as a missionary he would present his Christian theology as a contrasting and superior world view. Kraft made the point that in effect his colleague was simply arguing that American culture was better than the local African culture and he found this to be unacceptable. In contrast Kraft argued that translation must look for places of common concern and expression between cultures.[16a]

Kraft's description of the way that his missionary colleague interacted with the local Nigerian culture was deeply significant for me in my own work as a youth minister. I recognized that there was a sense in which the Church in my own context tended to reproduce the cultural imperialism of the missionaries when it tried to interact with the wider culture inhabited by many young people. The default setting seemed to be to present faith and the cultural expression of the Church as being superior to popular culture. I realized that if we were to find ways to share faith with young people like Kes, Chris and Charlie, then our starting point needed to be based on a deep appreciation and respect for their cultural world and it was only from this kind of understanding that a relevant expression of faith and church might emerge.

My commitment to a particular kind of practice had led me to an appreciation of the central importance of culture to practical theology. Culture was the key not simply to understanding the young people I was working with but also to understanding the expression of the Church. My interest in cultural studies as a key dialogue partner for

---

15 Kraft, *Christianity*, p. 6.
16 and 16a Kraft, *Christianity*, p. 7.

practical theology has grown from this realization. Cultural studies not only offered ways of understanding and interpreting young people and youth culture, but it also gave me insights into the wider popular culture. Cultural studies helped me to explore the way that popular culture had shaped my own life. At the same time it gave me tools to understand the way that the contemporary Church has embraced aspects of this culture, while at the same time rejecting others. What emerged was a realization that the culture of the Christian community was itself shaped as a reaction to the wider popular culture. Being Christian had become a 'taste culture' in the context of other taste cultures.[17] This means that the missiological task of translation in Western culture is made more complex because it is not so much translation from one community or ethnically or geographically located culture to another, but it involved communication of faith between subcultural groups within our own society.[18] Thus there are similarities and differences that come from the close relationship between people who live in the same city or are exposed to the same media. Moreover, I began to see that church culture, just like youth culture was a place for belonging and identity formation within the flow of the wider popular culture.[19] Kraft realized that the translation of faith in Africa meant that he had to be both an anthropologist and a theologian. The challenges that I faced as a youth minister required the ability to reflect both theologically and culturally. In the Western context, translation led me to explore an interdisciplinary approach to practical theology that made use of ways of seeing derived from cultural studies rather than anthropology.

Youth Culture and Cultural Studies

As a youth worker I had been drawn to young people who were into making music and starting their own rock bands. My youth work was based on the relationships that grew up around bands that were

17 For 'taste culture' see Thornton, S. (1995), *Club Cultures*, Cambridge: Polity Press.

18 For more on the theory of subcultures and the idea of taste culture see Gelder, K. and Thornton, S. (eds) (1997), *The Subcultures Reader*, London: Routledge.

19 See Ward, P. (2002), *Liquid Church*, Peabody: Henrickson/Carlisle: Paternoster, p. 27; see also Baumann, Z. (2000), *Liquid Modernity*, Cambridge: Polity Press, pp. 82ff.

rehearsing and doing gigs. It was the 1980s and Oxford was gripped by the vivid world of the Goth. Many of the guys in these bands had adopted Goth style and were much given to dressing in black, wearing eyeliner and back-combing their dyed hair. They looked rather outlandish and at that time they seemed to be a long way from the music, style and social world of the local churches. As I got to know and like these young people I also started to read cultural studies because it offered interpretative frameworks for understanding the cultural world that they inhabited. In particular it drew my attention to the way that youth cultures were formed out of an interaction between media-based popular culture and the creative social world and identities of young people.

One of the writers I found particularly helpful at this time was Paul Willis. Willis is perhaps unusual within cultural studies in that he has been committed to ethnographic research.[20] In *Common Culture* he explores the way that young people are active in creating their own meaning through popular forms of artistic creativity and expression. Willis called this symbolic creativity 'necessary work'.[21] For Willis, 'symbolic creativity is not only part of everyday human activity, but is also a necessary part. This is because it is an integral part of necessary work – that which is done every day, that which is not extra but essential to ensure the daily production and reproduction of human existence'.[21a] Interestingly he links this idea of necessary work to the theories of the Christian artist Eric Gill. Willis points out that for Gill the symbolic work involved in the reproduction of daily life was something that was holy. This idea that young people through participation in a creative interaction with a media-based culture might in some way be mediating 'holiness' was very helpful. It opened up a way that I could think theologically about everyday practices and cultures.

Willis highlights the way that young people are engaged in meaning-making. They do this through quite ordinary activities such as how they decorate their bedroom walls, or how they choose to wear their hair or even how they walk and stand. Meaning-making was important because it was necessary. People have to make meaning because life is impossible without meaning. Being active in making meaning

---

20 See Willis, P. (1977), *Common Culture*, Milton Keynes: Open University Press.
21 and 21a Willis, *Common*, p. 9.

is a kind of work but it is also in some sense 'holy'. What this implied for me was that the daily lives of the young people were not just an object for theological reflection and problematizing. Rather the symbolic creativity of young people was itself a place of theological creativity. In other words, the social and cultural world of the young people I had got to know could be seen as a starting point for the kind of mission studies based around translation that I had come across through the work of Charles Kraft and others.

If the challenge was one of translation I needed to find some point of connection or starting point for theological work. Given the interests of the young people I knew it was natural that this should be in music. My interest in popular music as a place for theological reflection was first sparked when I came across James Cone's book *The Spirituals and Blues*.[22] Against a more common sacred/secular interpretation of black music, Cone suggests that it is not just the spirituals that should be regarded as theological. He argues that, 'the blues are "secular spirituals." They are *secular* in the sense that they confine their attention solely to the immediate and affirm the bodily expression of the black soul, including its sexual manifestations. They are *spirituals* because they are impelled by the same search for the truth of black experience.'[23] So for Cone, theological expression of African Americans was not restricted to the spiritual – it was also to be found in the music of Muddy Waters, B. B. King and Robert Johnson.

Cone's approach to the theological reading of 'secular' music suggested ways to interpret the music of contemporary young people in the UK. Just as the blues might be an alternative spiritual music that operated outside of the Church, so also forms of hip hop or dance music or indie music might be similarly understood. Combined with Willis's idea of necessary work this approach to music suggested that it might be thought of as a place for meaning-making that might include the theological and the spiritual. So maybe the Goth style and music that I had met in the young people of Oxford should be seen as some kind of necessary theological work. The parallels between the rather dark sounds and inclinations of the young people I knew and early American blues was not as far-fetched as perhaps it might seem.

---

22 Cone, J. (1972), *The Spirituals and Blues*, New York: Seabury Press.
23 Cone, *Spirituals*, p. 112; italics retained.

After all, didn't Robert Johnson famously talk about going down to the crossroads and selling his soul to the devil?

The idea of necessary theological work raises some quite fundamental questions that relate to media and mediation in popular culture. The way of seeing derived from cultural studies deals with popular culture as the action of producers, the meaning of texts and the way that these texts are made use of by audiences. If youth culture is to be understood as necessary theological work then it must involve an exploration of theology and how it is operative in the interaction of all these levels of mediation. The theoretical discussion in this book is my attempt to understand practical theology as a reflection upon the way that media and mediation understood through this way of seeing affect the understanding of theological expression and ecclesial identity.

Youth Church

For me as a youth worker the relationship between the Church and mediation became one of the most pressing issues I had to face. As I have said, I found within a relatively short space of time that some of the young people I had got to know were interested in exploring the Christian faith. Because I was mainly working with rock bands it seemed most natural to try and find a way for them to use music as a form of theological expression. Within a few months some of the young people had written songs expressing their own understanding of the Christian faith. We used to meet up once a week to sing these songs together. What emerged was a rather rough and ready form of Christian worship. At the time I had a very small office but nevertheless we would set up the full band with drum kit, bass and electric guitar. Ten or fifteen of us would cram into this space and pass around a microphone as we sang the songs. Now and then we would read short passages from the Bible. All of this took place in the fug created by the cigarette smoke of the young people.[24]

We were already gathering together for a simple form of worship using the songs that young people had written. This practice of worship needed to relate to the ongoing life of the Christian community.

---

24 For a much fuller account of this see Ward, *Worship*.

The problem was how to develop this relationship with Church while avoiding the kind of disconnection and cultural dislocation experienced by Kes and his friends. As I was working through these questions I became aware of the Nine O'Clock Service in Sheffield. NOS, as it was to be known, had developed as a service of worship led by and for a group of young adults from the local club scene.[25] In a few years similar experimental worship services and congregations had been spawned all around the UK, and what became known as alternative worship was born.[26] The key move, from my perspective, represented by NOS and the other alternative worship groups was that they demonstrated how a regular worship service could become recognized by local churches and the wider Christian community as a legitimate form of 'Church'. This move was to eventually give rise to the Fresh Expressions movement in the UK and the Emerging Church in the USA.

Central to these various forms of ecclesial experimentation was the realization that changes in the wider 'popular' culture had created a momentum for new forms of Church. My own ministerial experience has meant that I have been very much concerned with the future shape of the Church. In *Liquid Church* I argued that changes in contemporary culture meant that the Church must become more fluid and liquid in form.[27] Central to the idea of ecclesial fluidity is the role that mediation plays in producing and circulating theological expression. Participation in a mediated ecclesial culture extends the Church and animates it to move beyond traditional frameworks. In finding ways to reflect on the theological significance of mediation, practical theology forms a part of these contemporary changes in the Church.[28]

---

25 The story of the Nine O'Clock Service in Sheffield is deeply tragic. An account of how it blazed brightly and much too fiercely for those involved can be found in Howard, R. (1996), *The Rise and Fall of the Nine O'Clock Service*, London: Mowbray.

26 For an account of the early development of alternative worship in the UK see Roberts, P. (1999), *Alternative Worship in the Church of England*, Nottingham: Grove Books.

27 Ward, *Liquid*.

28 See Ward, *Liquid*; Cray, G. (2004), *From Here to Where? The Culture of the Nineties*, Board of Mission Occasional Papers, 3, London: Board of Mission; Archbishops' Council, *Mission Shaped Church: Church Planting and Fresh Expressions of Church in a Changing Context*, London: Church House Publishing; and Riddell, M. (1998), *The Threshold of the Future: Reforming the Church in the Post-Christian West*, London: SPCK.

Reflexivity and Theology

Auto/theobiography shows how practical theology can be an embodied theology. Embodied in the sense that it has grown from my own practice as a youth minister. The auto/theobiographical method suggests that theological reflection and cultural expression coexist in biography and practice. This insight is a key point of reference in that it situates theological thought within the cultural and the experiential. At the same time this approach to reflexivity shows how theological and faith commitments can shape practical theology. So auto/theobiography generates practical theology that is culturally located but it is at the same time theologically committed. This inevitably raises a question concerning the relationship between theology and culture.

In qualitative research methodology and cultural studies, reflexivity is seen as an alternative to the notion that researchers are somehow detached from their study. As Johnson, Chambers, Rahuram and Tincknell say, 'There is no all-seeing god-like position available to us, no stance free from society, culture and power. This applies to everyone. We can, however, recognize existing forms of partiality and advance by dialogue especially, beyond them, arriving at better, but still partial knowledges.'[29]

If there is no 'god-like' position to view the cultural then what does this do to my theological commitments? One approach would be to locate theological commitment within the cultural as an aspect of expression and communal life. Susan Mizruchi touches on this issue when she says that the study of religion and religious culture must account for the fact that religious belief and practices are distinctive precisely because they claim to be in some way beyond culture.[30] Thus in adopting a cultural studies approach to the study of religion, she argues that there must be room made for the 'anomalous'. Such an approach, she says, acts as a 'disruptive classification'. This disruptive classification interrogates 'earlier modes of classification regarding religion and culture while at the same time developing categories for capturing what was mystified (as opposed to specified in contemporary theory) and

---

29 Johnson, *Practice*, p. 52.

30 Mizruchi, S. (2001), *Religion and Cultural Studies*, Princeton: Princeton University Press, p. xii.

unified (as opposed to fractured or fragmented in historical practice)'.[31] Mizruchi is saying that a cultural understanding of religion must have space within it for anomaly or a disruptive classification. The cultural study of religion must be open to mystery to allow for what might be beyond the realm of cultural theory.

I very much appreciate the way that Mizruchi approaches the cultural study of religion. Her sense that religious studies needs to make a space for the transcendent is based on a respectful and reflexive approach to the study of religion as a limited and self-limiting account of religious life. Yet disruption and anomaly only serve to situate the theological within a dominant cultural frame. This is a generous positioning of the theological, but it remains a positioning. For John Milbank this kind of positioning is an inevitability in the relationship between theology and social theory.

In *Theology and Social Theory* Milbank argues that theology either positions, or is in turn positioned by, secular discourses.[32] The timidity of theology has meant that it has frequently borrowed a 'fundamental account of society and history' and then sought theological insights which 'cohere with it'.[33] This enterprise is mistaken, he argues, because no such account, which is 'neutral, rational and universal' exists.[34] In these circumstances, says Milbank, theology must itself act as an account of the social. This involves a fundamental shift in what it means to think theologically. So Milbank argues that

> the claim here is not that theology, conceived in broadly traditional fashion, can now add to its competence certain new, 'social' pronouncements. On the contrary the claim is that *all* theology has to reconceive itself as a kind of 'Christian Sociology:' that is to say as the explication of a socio-linguistic practice, or as the re-narration of this practice as it has historically developed.[35]

---

31 Mizruchi, *Religion*, p. xii.
32 Milbank, J. (1990), *Theology and Social Theory: Beyond Secular Reason*, Oxford: Blackwell, p. 1.
33 Milbank, *Theology*, p. 380.
34 Milbank, *Theology*, p. 380.
35 Milbank, *Theology*, p. 381.

The impact of Milbank's intervention in theological discussion on the social sciences and questions of culture has been immense. At a very crude level the erudition and complexity of Milbank's *Theology and Social Theory* has been used by some as an excuse to ignore the social sciences or at least be very cautious and suspicious in their use.[36] My reading of Milbank, however, is that his suggestion that theology must be reconceived as a re-narration of practice located in the historical serves to locate belief in the cultural. At the same time he is clear that situating the theological in this way must not reduce the theological to the cultural.

Mizruchi is arguing, from within the discipline of religious studies, that while religion can be understood and interpreted as a cultural phenomenon it must not be reduced to this analysis. Her acceptance that there must be a space made for mystery challenges the notion that there is a detached and all-seeing position in relation to the religious. Such a position is problematic precisely because it runs the risk of missing what lies at the heart of what is being described, that is, the religious conviction that there is a God and that this God is not necessarily contained by the cultural. Milbank from a quite different position is arguing that social theory has tended to position and reduce Christian belief and theology to the social and the cultural. Theologians, he points out, have had a tendency to adopt reductive descriptions of faith and then seek to find ways to adapt theology to the secular accounts of belief. Milbank argues that belief is situated in the history and practices of the Church and as a result theology must be reconceived as a narration of this practice. At the same time, such a re-narration must foreground its commitments and the way that the theological situates cultural analysis and understandings. I am very much in sympathy with the direction of Milbank's thinking but I am a little uneasy with an argument that seems to deal with the theological and the social as a relationship between disciplines and theories. Theology clearly relates to a rational discourse but it is much more than that.

---

36 See Cartledge, M. (2003), *Practical theology: Charismatic and Empirical Perspectives*, Carlisle: Paternoster, p. 1; reference is to note in Cartledge, p. 32.

Participation

Studying theology at university left me confused. It was when still at school that I first realized that I should pursue a future in Christian ministry. I talked to the vicar and had a few exploratory conversations with my diocese about ordination.[37] The plan was that I would read theology with a mind to eventually offering myself for ordination. So in October 1977 I was a bright and bushy-tailed undergraduate making the daily trek to lectures in the theology department next door to the cathedral in Durham.

Theology at Durham was heady stuff. The department was in one of its glory periods. C. K. Barrett lectured us on John's Gospel and C. E. B. Cranfield on Romans, and I read Calvin's Institutes with the saintly T. H. L. Parker. A young Stephen Sykes had just been appointed as a professor of systematic theology and alongside the great men (with and without initials) we had seminars on the philosophy of religion with Ann Loades. I loved it but it did leave me just a little puzzled. I think I had signed up to a theology degree with a notion that it would help me in my chosen path of ministry. I don't think I was entirely alone in thinking that way. Most of my contemporaries were studying because they planned to go on to some kind of Christian ministry. In fact in the second year our numbers were significantly boosted by Anglican ordinands from Cranmer Hall as well as by students training for the Catholic priesthood at Ushaw College.

So we were all studying theology as part of our preparation for ministry, but this seemed to be the elephant in the room. The lectures were wonderful, but they rarely if ever made any connection to ministerial practice. In fact, as students, we were actively discouraged from any attempt to relate our studies to practice or spirituality. The interesting thing was that all of the lecturers in the theology department at that time, in their different ways, were clearly committed to the Church and its ministry. Most were ordained or active in their denominations and some of the professors were even canons at the cathedral. Even more curious was the general sense that went through the department that

---

37 I should probably say that I am not ordained. Looking back I think the reason was that ordained ministry didn't at the time seem to be a way to do what I felt called to do, that is, work with young people, but I suppose it would not be unfair to say that there is a sense in which youth ministry inoculated me against it!

the study of theology was something that was deeply significant for the life of the Church. What we were doing was ecclesially important and yet at the same time there was a severe reluctance to make connections between the various areas of specialist knowledge that made up the undergraduate programme in theology and ministerial practice.[38]

I left Durham with a real love of theology and a conviction that I had been given a glimpse of something wonderful that was crucially important. At the same time I really had no idea how to make sense of it all in relation to my calling as a youth minister. As I continued to work with young people I found that cultural studies gave me an understanding of the issues I was facing and missiology helped me to make the connection between culture and faith, but paradoxically although theology was my first love, and I continued to read in the field, I genuinely struggled to find ways to build fruitful connections between my ministry and the biblical studies, church history and systematic theology I had been introduced to in Durham.

I don't think I was alone in this kind of disconnection. In fact as Elaine Graham, Heather Walton and Frances Ward point out, a sense of dislocation from traditional forms of theological thought is quite common in practical theology. They suggest that the vogue

> within many parts of adult theological education for encouraging students to 'reflect theologically' has suffered from a lack of rigour. In its emphasis on the immediate imperatives of ministry, it proceeds with no clear idea how traditional Christian sources such as Scripture are to be handled; it lacks proper integration with other fields of scholarship such as biblical studies, systematic theology and the history of Christianity; and it does not equate its own contemporary practice of reflection with similar processes that have given rise to theological discourse throughout Christian history.[39]

I very much identify with these sentiments.

---

38 At Durham there was one rather unexpected connection between theology and youth ministry. This was occasioned by John Rogerson, who lectured us on the Pentateuch. The lectures were unusual in that they were scheduled for 5 p.m. The first evening we realized why. Rogerson turned up dressed in scout uniform. He was a keen member of the scouts and after the lecture he was leading a group somewhere in the city. So JDE and P was presented to us with a definite whiff of the sheep shank and dib, dib, dob!

39 Graham, E., Walton, H. and Ward, F. (2007), *Theological Reflection: Sources*, London: SCM Press, p. 1.

During the mid 1980s I was involved in setting up a training course for Christian youth workers.[40] The idea was that we would design a form of theological education that was based around an apprenticeship model of learning. Students would learn as they did youth ministry working alongside a more experienced practitioner. This approach to training I would say was very much in danger of reproducing some of the problems identified by Graham, Walton and Ward in that it was not entirely obvious how students should interact with more traditional forms of theology.

It was around this time that I made one of my periodic pilgrimages back to Durham. While I was there I stumbled across a book written by my old Patristics lecturer, George Dragas. In *The Meaning of Theology* Dragas explores the development of the idea of theology in Greek patristic thought from the apologists to its culmination in the Cappadocian fathers.[41] Dragas shows how the fathers, drawing upon Greek philosophy, understood reason to be a spiritual engagement. This idea of the spiritual nature of thought was brought together with a revelatory understanding of the knowledge of God that the fathers found in the Hebrew Bible.[42] So Dragas argues that for Origen knowledge of God is a spiritual rationality. True knowledge, in Origen's thinking, is communicated by God, and the 'supreme instance' of this communication is the gospel.[43] This 'true' and 'spiritual' knowledge is rooted in a mystical dialogue of encounter. 'The knowledge of God is his bosom in which he places and holds all the god-minding persons as if they were his gold which he keeps in his bosom.'[44] Here in Origen's writing theology becomes an intimate encounter, a divine cradling. It is not so much that rationality and enquiry is replaced by spirituality, rather it is taken up and transformed through a mystical intimacy or dialogue.[45] Dragas goes on to suggest that in Athanasius' thinking the link between rationality and spirituality is found in the being of God. Thus in the 'First Oration against the Arians' Athanasius says that 'Theology

---

40 The training course was called Oxford Youth Works.
41 Dragas, G. (1980), *The Meaning of Theology: An Essay in Greek Patristics*, Darlington: Darlington Carmel.
42 Dragas, *Meaning*, p. 83.
43 Dragas, *Meaning*, p. 17.
44 Origen, quoted in Dragas, *Meaning*, p. 17.
45 Dragas, *Meaning*, p. 18.

is perfect (complete) in the Trinity. This is the only true piety and this is the good and the truth.'[46] Dragas argues that piety in this context relates to ideas of revelation found in the Hebrew scriptures whereas the 'good' and the 'true' draw upon Hellenic philosophy. The key point is that it is the being of God as Trinity that positions and structures these two as theology. The connection between theology and Trinity, according to Didymus the Blind, is linked to an encounter with divine power. So 'God's theology is his power, and his glory and indeed his energy which does wonders.'[47]

Dragas argues that the understanding of theology as a spiritual rationality that is based in an encounter with God who is Trinity finds its culmination in the Cappadocian fathers. For the Cappadocians theology as encounter becomes participation in divine glory through worship or doxology. So Gregory of Nyssa says:

> I speak of one Godhood; for that Godhood which I see in the Father I also see in the Son; and that which I see in the Holy Spirit I also see in the Son because there is one form of both ... and so there is one worship and one doxology rendered by us ... i.e. one true theology; you have one glory ... that you may not divide the worship and therefore divide the Godhood into many gods.[48]

So theology is positioned by God who is Trinity, and to speak or think about God, says Dragas, is not merely human talk, 'because it involves the reception of the mind of God and the participation in the life of God'.[49] To do theology is to be taken up into the realm of worship and glory. It is this patristic theology of participation, worship and glory that forms the basis for my understanding of practical theology.

Perichoresis and Theology

It was probably significant that I came across this patristic approach to theology on a visit back to Durham. I was just setting out on my journey

---

46 Athanasius, quoted in Dragas, *Meaning*, p. 28.
47 Dragas, *Meaning*, p. 38.
48 Gregory of Nyssa, quoted in Dragas, *Meaning*, p. 69.
49 Dragas, *Meaning*, p. 70.

as a theological educator. Spending time back where I was a student gave me an opportunity to process the experience of being an undergraduate. Theological study had left me conflicted. I had learned to have a deep regard for the Christian tradition and its ways of reasoning in relation to the Bible, church history and doctrine, but I was finding it hard to see how this field of knowledge made sense in relation to my work as a youth worker. Now with the task of designing a training course for Christian youth workers I was determined that I would not reproduce the kind of dislocation between practice and academic theology that I had been introduced to in my undergraduate studies. At the same time I wanted to pass on a love for study and for the tradition of the Church.

With Dragas as my guide I caught a glimpse from the fathers of a way forward, and it involved a shift in what was meant by 'theology'. From Origen and Athanasius I learned that theology was not simply an academic discipline or a form of secular reasoning. Thinking and speaking about God was not the same as other kinds of rationality. For the fathers theological knowledge mediated the life of God. It is significant that this approach to theology is mystical and spiritual in and through the processes of reasoning. So the intimate encounter of theology in the 'bosom' of God is simultaneously human dialogue and expression. Dragas helped me to start to make sense of my previous academic work not by rejecting it but by investing it with a much deeper significance. These insights were really helpful as I set about developing a training programme for youth workers where, if I am honest, the temptation was always to be drawn towards a pragmatic and largely cultural approach to 'what works' with young people. The challenge from the fathers was to find a way to inform and transform this kind of experiential and practice-based training. The way forward did not involve the rejection of traditional forms of theological reasoning in favour of the experiential but an understanding of theology as an encounter with God. In other words there was a link between theological reasoning and the practice of worship and prayer.

I should probably say that this way of thinking has not come easily to me and it has taken me a while to assimilate the kind of patristic theology that I first came across in Dragas's work. My own journey into a participative Trinitarian theology has been informed not so much by reading learned works on the Trinity as by the experience of prayer and worship. Early on in my Christian life I was introduced to contemplative forms of prayer by reading Anthony Bloom's *School for Prayer*.[50] Bloom presented Orthodox spirituality in a way that I found both accessible and profound. This form of prayer helped me to explore a spirituality that was based on resting and being present in the presence of God. It was a practice of dwelling in God and of also being indwelt by God. There was something about this kind of prayer that was new to me, but it was also very familiar. As an evangelical Christian I had been led to faith by 'inviting Jesus into my heart' and as a charismatic I had explored a spirituality that was based on the baptism and fullness of the Spirit. My journey to an evangelical conversion and then a subsequent charismatic experience had introduced me to a Christian spirituality which out of its own integrity was participatory in nature. As a result, although it was a different kind of spiritual practice, I never saw Bloom's approach of prayer as different or alien to my own tradition. Contemplative prayer was merely a way of entering into my evangelical and charismatic spirituality more fully.

So in a variety of ways my spiritual practice was shaped around a theology of being indwelt by the Holy Spirit. I understood the Christian life and therefore my ministry among young people as a spiritual practice of abiding or dwelling in the life of God. This participative theology had formed me as a Christian and as a minister, but it operated as an embodied knowledge. It has only been through reflexivity that this embodied theology has started to resonate for me with the kind of Trinitarian thought found in the Greek fathers. Patristic theology helped me to make a link between my spiritual experience and my love of theology as an academic discipline. It is this connection that informs my understanding of practical theology as participation and mediation. Through participation practical theology becomes a discipline of prayerful encounter with God. One of the key reasons for this is that 'theology' mediates the presence of God. By theology I do not just mean the discipline of academic reasoning in relation to particular texts and traditions. Theology also relates to the words, images, metaphors and symbolic ways of being that circulate in a variety of ways in the expression of the Church.

---

50 Bloom, A. (1971), *School for Prayer*, London: DLT.

Participation in God and Mission

The insight that 'theology' is active as a mediation of the divine life can be extended to the practice of ministry. The style of youth work that I had started to explore was based on finding ways to build relationships with young people outside of formal church-based meetings and programmes. This kind of youth work is fairly challenging. It was terrifying to go to the local high school and try to make connections with young people that I did not know and in what seemed at first to be a closed world. In the early 1980s most Christian youth work was set up so that young people had to come onto church territory. This was a context where adults felt comfortable and the leaders set the ground rules. Of course the downside of this was that only some young people were willing to come to church meetings. The style of relational ministry that I was attempting aimed to turn all of this upside down. I set myself the task of journeying into the world of young people and meeting them in situations where they felt at home. The idea was that I went to their territory. This meant that I was a visitor in a context where they were in control and they set the rules. Needless to say this was not at all easy, but interestingly almost from the start I felt that this kind of ministry was a deeply spiritual practice. Going to young people, rather than asking them to come to me, gave me a strong sense that I was in some way sharing in God's love and concern for the world. In fact more than that, I was struck by the conviction that the Holy Spirit was there with the young people even before I arrived. So I wasn't just meeting young people, there was also a sense in which I was meeting God. This was a God who seemed at times to be saying, 'Where have you been? What took you so long to get here?' This approach to ministry felt very much like I was simply answering a call to join a God who was, like me, simply 'being there'. Here was a God who was passionately engaged in being present among these young people whether they came to church or not. This experience of youth ministry as a participation in God's active presence in the world has influenced my understanding of the doctrine of the Trinity.

Paul Fiddes makes a connection between a theology of participation and what he calls 'the dance of God'.[51] He argues that by the end of the

---

51 Fiddes, P. (2000), *Participating in God: A Pastoral Doctrine of the Trinity*, London: DLT, p. 71.

fourth century the fathers in both the East and the West saw the nature of God as a communion of persons. The relation of these persons was eventually referred to as 'perichoresis'. Perichoresis carried the meaning of the mutual indwelling, exchange and penetration of persons.[52] So Fiddes says, 'the term "perichoresis" thus expresses the permeation of each person by the other, their coinherence without confusion. It takes up and develops the words of Jesus in the Fourth Gospel: "believe me that I am in the Father and the Father is in me". (Jn 4:11)'.[53] Perichoresis has long been associated with the idea of dance. For Fiddes the image of the divine dance represents patterns of relationship that are so intimate that the dancers do not simply move alongside and around one another but they dance in and through each other.[54] In the Church this Trinitarian dance is participatory, with believers in community joining in the dance of God.

Fiddes's discussion of perichoresis as a participatory engagement in the dancing life of God has helped me to understand the connection between my own experience of ministry and participation in the Trinitarian life of God. My sense that relational ministry involved joining in with God's loving presence among young people is akin to the notion of an inclusive dance. Yet here this dance is extended beyond the Christian community into a missional engagement with the world. So participation means that there is a coming together in practical theology of academic rationality, the practice of contemplative prayer and mission. I learned that journeying to be with young people was 'theology' in that it was an encounter with the life of God. By participating in relational mission I was joining in the missional dance of the Trinity. In and through my action as a minister I was dwelling in and being indwelt by the life of God. The action of ministry was participation but it was also mediation. My choices about how I did ministry mediated the divine presence. This was not the usual kind of evangelistic communication from the minister to the non-churched, rather it was a mediation of the life of God to the minister through the act of ministering.

---

52 Fiddes, *Participating*, p. 71.
53 Fiddes, *Participating*, p. 71.
54 Fiddes, *Participating*, p. 72.

Auto/theobiography, and Practical Theology as Participation and Mediation

This exercise in reflexivity has introduced the key themes that I continue to develop throughout this book.

Part 1, Converging on Culture, focuses on the relationship between theology and culture. Chapter 1 discusses the way that practical theology has developed as part of wider dialogue within modern theology. Chapter 2 continues this discussion through an examination of mission studies and contextualization. Chapter 3 introduces key themes in cultural studies as a way of seeing that can inform practical theology. This way of seeing is developed further in the next chapter through a discussion of cultural studies and approaches to the study of popular music. These perspectives are illustrated through an analysis of a contemporary worship song written by Graham Kendrick, 'Shine, Jesus, Shine'.

Part 2, Participation and Mediation, returns to a Trinitarian theology. Chapter 5 situates practical theology as a spiritual practice of reflected and transforming glory. The idea of mediation as a theological and cultural category is developed in more depth in Chapter 6. This leads on in Chapter 7 to a discussion of the communion as participation and mediation.

Part 3, Liquid Church and a Consuming Faith, explores the ecclesial implications of mediation through a discussion of the way that the contemporary Church makes use of consumer culture. Chapter 8 deals with the material culture of contemporary Christianity. Chapter 9 locates this material culture in the productive processes of the Christian culture industry. The final chapter focuses on the way that mediation as 'flow' acts to extend and make ecclesial being more fluid.

Part 1

Converging On Culture

I

Practical Theology

Ministers often experience practical theology as counter-intuitive and sometimes even as alienating. This is odd because on the face of it practical theology is concerned with finding ways to reconcile practice and theory. The problem is that this is presented largely as an academic issue. In contrast, practitioners come to theological education with a faith that is embodied or lived in. Most of us have learned how to think, pray, worship, teach and preach within our church context. We find ourselves in ministerial education because we have been recognized as having certain skills in these areas. Being called to the ministry (be that ordained or some form of lay ministry) means that we are already a participant in the flow of expression and reasoning within a tradition and community. In our church context and in our ministerial practice doctrine and experience are held together as part of being a believer in a community of faith. When we pray, sing hymns, make decisions about life, preach and teach, and so on, we inhabit our theology. It is the process of education, however, that seeks to tease this embodied expression apart. As Edward Farley has argued, theological education 'atomizes' subject areas and fragments theological unity.[55] So theological education tends to socialize practitioners into the view that there is a problem in relating experience and theology.

Practical theology as an academic discipline has developed as a conversation shaped around different kinds of correlational or mediating methodologies. At the heart of this conversation lies a series of related questions concerning the interaction of a range of opposing 'dualisms'. So practical theology has generally been framed as a way

---

55 Farley, E. (1983), *Theologia: The Fragmentation and Unity of Theological Education*, Philadelphia: Fortress Press, p. 4.

of mediating between, or correlating, experience and revelation, practice and theory, social science and doctrine. This academic orientation towards practical theology as a discipline based on reconciling dualisms tracks a much wider debate concerning the relationship between modernity and theology. Practical theology forms a part of this larger theological discussion concerning doctrine and human experience. This chapter explores the theoretical shape of practical theology as part of modern theology. The various methodologies of mediation and correlation in practical theology and in modern theology are seen as developing a parallel trajectory towards a point of convergence around the question of culture and faith as a form of communal practice. The move toward practice and culture is of particular importance for the ministerial practitioner because the convergence on culture offers a way forward to a less fragmented kind of practical theology. So the point here is that culture as a category opens the field for a less alienating kind of theology.

The Pastoral Cycle

One of the key ways that practical theology has sought to structure theological reflection has been through what has been called the pastoral cycle.[56] Paul Ballard and John Pritchard present the cycle as a series of stages through which the practitioner must move to implement the methodology. These stages are: experience, exploration, reflection and action. In the first stage the present situation is seen as the starting point. Experience refers to the way that events produce or uncover a 'tension' to which there must be a response.[57] Exploration involves a systematic analysis of the situation. Reflection brings to bear values and questions of belief in relation to the information that has been gathered. Action is the point where changed patterns are brought into practice in the light of what has been learned through the process.[58] In many ways this method of reflection is a form of problem-solving

---

56 The pastoral cycle has many forms but here I will look at the way it is discussed in Ballard, P. and Pritchard, J. (1996), *Practical theology in Action: Christian Thinking in the Service of Church and Society*, London: SPCK.

57 Ballard and Pritchard, *Practical*, p. 77.

58 Ballard and Pritchard, *Practical*, pp. 77–8.

which offers a structured way to address the issues that commonly arise from ministerial practice. It does, however, raise some interesting questions in relation to the shape of practical theology.

The pastoral cycle tends to reinforce the dislocation between reflection and the everyday. This is perhaps ironic because the method is trying to do the opposite. The problem is that it separates both the analysis of a pastoral situation and theological reflection as particular stages in the method. Thus experience is effectively distanced or distilled through analytical moves. These different stages are manufactured as part of the method and they position the practitioner in a framework based on these distinctions. So in theological education the practitioner is taught that they should adopt this way of reflecting as the means to bring to bear theoretical and theological perspectives on a pastoral situation. Theological reflection has become established as a key methodology in practical theology but as Elaine Graham, Heather Walton and Frances Ward have pointed out, how the minister is to reflect theologically is often far from clear. They argue that despite its prevalence theological reflection is somewhat problematic.[59]

> Theological reflection is still easier said than done. Received understandings of theological reflection are largely under-theorized and narrow, and too often fail to connect adequately with biblical, historical and systematic scholarship.[60]

The mystery around theological reflection that the authors highlight comes in large part from the way that this kind of method creates stages that separate experience, analysis and reflection. The method is mysterious and alienating because it goes against the theological reflex of the practitioner.

In the practice of faith, doctrine is performed as it is prayed, sung, preached and enacted in mission. To be a person of faith means that the theological is embodied as lifestyle, belonging and identity. To live as a person of faith and as a minister is to inhabit or live in the doctrinal. In faith, theology is performed and practised as it is lived

---

59 Graham, E., Walton, H. and Ward, F. (2005), *Theological Reflection: Methods*, London: SCM Press, p. 1.
60 Graham, *Methods*, p. 1.

in. The modern dislocation between experience and doctrine and the subsequent methodologies of correlation as seen in the pastoral cycle are counter-intuitive for the practitioner because they present the cultural and the theological as two distinct worlds that must in some way be reconciled. In the pastoral cycle the practitioner is encouraged to refract experience through analytical categories that present the interpretation of a pastoral situation, and then the analysis and the reflection of faith upon this situation, as distinct moments in a method. Then as a result of these dislocated stages of thought the practitioner is faced with the challenge of forming a unity out of what has been made separate by the process. So a complex lived situation has been dissected and ministers can very often find themselves feeling like a child who has taken the clock apart, scratching their heads as to which piece goes where.

The problem with the pastoral cycle owes a great deal to the debates that have been raging in the theological world more generally concerning the relationship between experience and theology, practice and theory. The shape of practical theology has emerged in dialogue with other forms of theological thought as they have struggled to come to terms with modernity. So the tensions felt by practitioners as they attempt to implement the methods of the pastoral cycle, and other approaches developed by practical theology, have in large part echoed those expressed by systematic theologians as they sought to develop methodologies that take account of modernity. Before looking in more detail at practical theology we therefore need to turn to this wider conversation within modern theology.

Theology and Modernity

To get to the heart of the tension felt by ministers confronted with the fragmenting tendencies in practical theology it is necessary to examine the way that theology in general has attempted to come to terms with modern thought. Practical theology has developed in relation to these much larger and more wide-ranging theological debates within modernity. David Ford suggests that modern theology as a whole should be set within the context of what he calls 'reductionist and naturalist' accounts of religion. Ford says that the modern intellectual landscape has been shaped by the work of figures such as Feuerbach in philosophy, Marx in politics and economics, Durkheim and Weber in sociology, Frazer on comparative religion, William James in psychology, Darwin in evolutionary biology, and Nietzsche in philosophy.[61] These thinkers represent a pattern in thinking about religion that ranges beyond a particular academic discipline. This pattern, says Ford, forms part of the 'common sense' of many twentieth-century educated Western people.[62]

Modern theology can be seen as a series of different positions or types of response to this 'common sense'. Each type represents a different relationship to the intellectual environment which characterizes modernity. Ford suggests that there are five types of modern theology and it is possible to situate these types in relation to each other as if they form a line or continuum. At one end of this continuum 'type one' is characterized by the attempt to repeat a traditional expression of faith. It sees all reality within its own terms, 'with no recognition of the significance for it of other perspectives or of all that has happened in recent centuries'.[63] The fifth type, at the opposing end of the continuum, is characterized, according to Ford, by a dominant philosophy, which serves to assess and express, solely within its own terms, all theological expression. He excludes both of these types from consideration in his survey of modern theology. The first is excluded because it is 'hardly modern' and the fifth because it is 'hardly Christian'.[64] This leaves him with three basic types of theology, which fall within his treatment of major theologians. Type two gives priority to the self-description of the Church. It sees reality in relation to this self-description. Christian identity is 'primary', yet faith must be continually rethought and in doing so it must engage seriously with the 'modern world'.[65] Ford suggests that the leading figure in this type is Karl Barth. Type three represents a middle path. This is the method

---

61 Ford, D. (ed.) (2006), *The Modern Theologians* (3rd edn), Oxford: Blackwell, p. 8.

62 Ford, *Modern*, p. 8.

63 Ford, *Modern*, p. 2.

64 Ford, *Modern*, p. 2.

65 Ford, *Modern*, p. 2.

of correlation. Here traditional faith is brought into a dialogue with modernity. There is no 'over-arching integration' of Christianity and modernity within this type, says Ford, and neither would one be seen as being subsumed by the other. The theologian most associated with this type is Paul Tillich. In this type questions that are raised in life and thought are 'correlated' with answers developed from the Christian tradition.[66] Type four, says Ford, takes a particular philosophy and uses this to locate Christianity within modernity. Those working in this type of theology are concerned to do justice to both Christianity and modernity and they do this by developing a 'consistent reinterpretation of Christianity in terms of some contemporary idiom or concern'.[67]

Ford's presentation of modern theology is largely based on Hans Frei's five types of theology,[68] but this kind of typological approach to understanding the relationship between theology and modernity is also found in David Tracy's *Blessed Rage for Order*.[69] Tracy suggests that

---

66 Ford, *Modern*, p. 2.

67 Ford, *Modern*, p. 3.

68 Frei, H. (1992), *Types of Christian Theology*, New Haven: Yale University Press.

69 Tracy, D. (1975), *Blessed Rage for Order: The New Pluralism in Theology*, Chicago: Chicago University Press. Frei's types are numbered in reverse order to those of Ford. Type one: 'theology as a philosophical discipline' accords the prime place in theological discourse to philosophical categories (Frei, *Types*, p. 28). In Frei's fifth type Christian theology is seen as being exclusively the self-description of the Church. External categories such as those drawn from philosophy or from the social sciences have no bearing on this enterprise (Frei, *Types*, p. 4). Type two he identifies with Kant and Kaufman. Here theology, he says, is 'subsumed' under philosophical categories. It correlates Christian faith with 'general cultural meaning structures such as natural science or the "spirit" of a cultural era'. He sees liberal theologians such as Bultmann, Pannenberg and Tracy as examples of this type, but he also includes evangelicals such as Henry as following this method (Frei, *Types*, p. 3). Type three he identifies with Tillich and also with Schleiermacher. This type 'seeks to correlate theology as a procedure subject to formal, universal, and transcendental criteria for valid thinking with theology as a specific second order self description. It is distinct from type two in that it does not propose a "supertheory" or comprehensive structure for integrating them' (Frei, *Types*, p. 3). The fourth type argues that Christian theology is a non-systematic 'combination of normed Christian self-description and method founded on general theory' (Frei, *Types*, p. 3). This type is distinctive in that it does not treat the two as equal and equivalent partners and it reverses the order of priority compared to that of the second type. Here 'the practical discipline of Christian self description governs and limits the applicability of general criteria of meaning in theology' (Frei, *Types*, p. 4). Frei sees Karl Barth as the primary exponent of this type in the twentieth century. Newman in the nineteenth century, says Frei, and Edwards in the eighteenth century are also examples of this type.

this kind of theological typology is also to be found in the work of Ian Ramsey and Frederick Ferre.[70] The two ends of the continuum are represented by what Tracy calls orthodox theology and radical theology. For orthodox theology, says Tracy, 'the claims of modernity are not seen to have any inner theological relevance'. In fact a commitment to orthodox belief and expression is seen as a 'bulwark' against contemporary philosophy and criticism.[71] At the opposite extreme lies radical theology. Radical theologians are aware of liberal and neo-orthodox traditions; however, they have taken the crucial step, says Tracy, of applying the dialectic of neo-orthodoxy to faith itself. The result is a re-expression of the Christian tradition, 'which negates the central belief of that tradition in God'.[72] Tracy's major concern in presenting these five types of theology is to offer his own type. He calls this the 'revisionist model of critical correlation'. The revisionist theologian, says Tracy, is committed to the central task of contemporary theology: 'the dramatic confrontation, the mutual illuminations and corrections, the possible basic reconciliation between the principal values, cognitive claims, and existential faiths of both a reinterpreted post-modern consciousness and a reinterpreted Christianity'.[73] Tracy presents the two remaining types, liberal theology and neo-orthodox theology, as being in a close and interactive relationship with each other and also with revisionist theology.[74]

The typological device adopted by Tracy, Ford and others constructs theological debate around a central problem of relationship. The notion of types, as we have seen, creates a pattern where different kinds of theology are distributed along an imaginary linear continuum. At the poles of the continuum are two seemingly opposed positions and towards the centre there are types of theology which set out to reconcile these extremes. Recently a number of theologians, from different traditions and in different ways, have sought to reframe the modernist problematic of opposing irreconcilable poles. What their work has in common is a turn towards the cultural as a place of convergence.

---

70 Tracy, *Blessed*, p. 34 note.
71 Tracy, *Blessed*, p. 24.
72 Tracy, *Blessed*, p. 31.
73 Tracy, *Blessed*, p. 32.
74 Tracy, *Blessed*, p. 32–33.

Theology and the Turn to Culture

In *The Nature of Doctrine*[75] George Lindbeck argues that modern theology consists of two basic types. The first he calls the 'cognitive-propositional', where doctrine is seen as operating as a series of 'informative propositions or truth claims about objective realities'. This, he says, is the approach of traditional orthodoxies.[76] The second he labels the 'experiential-expressivist'. Here doctrine is seen as 'non-informative and non-discursive symbols of inner feelings, attitudes, or existential orientations'.[77] This approach, he says, characterizes liberal theology and it has its roots in the work of Schleiermacher. Between these two there are a number of theologies which seek to combine both the cognitive-propositional with the experiential-expressive.[78] Lindbeck, argues for what he calls a theological 'paradigm shift' away from models based around the experiential-expressivist and the cognitive-propositional. In their place he argues for a new approach based on what he calls a 'cultural-linguistic' model for religion.[79]

> Stated more technically, a religion can be viewed as a kind of cultural and/or linguistic framework or medium that shapes the entirety of life and thought. ... it is similar to an idiom that makes possible the description of realities, the formulation of beliefs and the experiencing of inner attitudes, feelings and sentiments.[80]

Kathryn Tanner, like Lindbeck, argues that culture and the cultural interact with theological discourse in crucial ways. A postmodern 'anthropological' view of culture, she says, has broken out of the disciplinary context of anthropology and influenced a range of academic work. Culture as an explanatory category has an importance that can be likened to the significance of categories such as 'gravity in physics, disease in medicine, or evolution in biology'.[81] Tanner's contention is

---

75 Lindbeck, G. (1984), *The Nature of Doctrine*, London: SPCK.
76 Lindbeck, *Nature*, p. 16.
77 Lindbeck, *Nature*, p. 16.
78 Lindbeck, *Nature*, p. 16.
79 Lindbeck, *Nature*, p. 9.
80 Lindbeck, *Nature*, p. 33.
81 Kroeber and Kluckhohn, quoted in Tanner, K. (1997), *Theories of Culture*, Minneapolis: Fortress Press, p. ix.

that this cultural perspective is potentially of considerable significance for theological thinking. The significance of the cultural is that it not only serves to locate theological work as a conversation concerning the practice and expression of the Church but it also identifies the activity of the theologian as itself a form of practice.[82] Tanner points out, however, that these concerns are not in themselves particularly unique. Theologians have always been concerned with the practice of faith. So there is a sense in which, for instance, very different theologians, such as Barth, or Schleiermacher, or liberation theologians, are all in their way interacting with the expression of the Church. What is innovative is the suggestion that these practices should be expressed in explicitly cultural terms.[83] While Tanner is not directly following Lindbeck's cultural-linguistic approach to religion she is taking up the shift towards the cultural. This shift to the cultural is echoed in the work of a number of theologians. Nicholas Healy's use of culture in relation to ecclesiology is a good example of this move.

Recent theological work on the Church, says Healy, has mostly been highly systematic and theoretical. At the same time this focus on theory has tended to avoid discussion of the 'rather messy, confused and confusing body that the Church actually is'.[84] The preference has been for theoretical consideration of what the Church should be rather than a consideration of it as a historic and concrete reality.[85] This concrete Church, he says, should not be understood in contradistinction to another spiritual or theological reality. Dealing with Church as concrete is not just a sociological task since the concrete Church is the locus for the activity of the Holy Spirit. Neither can the Church be dealt with in terms of the history of ideas or beliefs.

> Rather, it can be summarily described as a distinctive way of life, made possible by the gracious action of the Holy Spirit, which orients its adherents to the Father through Jesus Christ. By schooling its members, the Church makes that orientation a present possibility

---

82 Tanner, *Theories*, p. 72.

83 Tanner, *Theories*, p. 72.

84 Healy, N. (2000), *Church, World and the Christian Life*, Cambridge: Cambridge University Press, p. 3.

85 Healy, *Church*, p. 3; see also Scharen, C. (2005), '"Judicious Narratives", or Ethnography as Ecclesiology', *Scottish Journal of Theology* 58(2), pp. 125–42.

for them. The Christian way of life is distinctive because its Lord is a particular person and because its God is triune. Its life therefore takes a concrete form in the web of social practices accepted and promoted by the community as well as in the activities of its individual members.[86]

So Healy suggests that the Church may be best understood in terms of agency and activity, rather than ontology. It is the Holy Spirit which is active in the Church, and yet the identity of the Church is also made by human agency. It is constructed and reconstructed by 'the grace-enabled activities of its members as they embody the church's practices, beliefs and evaluations'.[87] Thus Healy sets out to avoid what he sees as theological and non-theological reductionism by describing the complex mix of agency and grace, Holy Spirit and embodied practices, which he calls the 'concrete Church'. He is concerned to distance his work from notions of correlation familiar from Niebuhr's *Christ and Culture* and more recently Tracy's *Analogical Imagination*. He points out that the weakness of these approaches in ecclesiology is that they assume that the two entities, Church and secular culture, can be described independently and then discussed in relation to each other. He argues that such an enterprise is not possible. The Church and its context are interconnected. Context here relates to a range of factors that shape and influence Christian witness. The concrete Church lives in the shifting and changing world and it is in particular contexts that it performs its tasks of witness and discipleship. Theological enquiry needs to shift its focus towards what he calls 'the critical theological analysis of these contexts and the present shape and activity of the Church within them'.[88]

Healy's discussion of the Church supports the notion that ministers live in and embody theology in their practice. Interestingly, the work of theologians such as Lindbeck, Tanner and Healy is evidence that theological conversation is undergoing something of a turn to culture. Sheila Greeve Davaney suggests that this turn or convergence on culture is a decisive shift in contemporary theology towards 'everyday

---

86 Healy, *Church*, p. 5.
87 Healy, *Church*, p. 5.
88 Healy, *Church*, p. 39.

beliefs and practices'.[89] She argues that, 'Broadly across the discipline of academic theology, there has been a move away from the study of ideas abstracted from their concrete histories and contexts and a turn to thick histories and realities of religious communities and individuals.'[90] At the same time, however, with Tanner, she points out that this shift also means that theologians are interpreting their own practices, politics and identities in cultural terms. 'Shorn of the illusion that we traffic with ahistorical and universal truth, theologians have been returned to what Linell Cady has aptly called the "morass" of lived religion.'[91] At the same time it is clear that the turn to culture should not involve the reduction of the theological to the cultural. So what these writers have in common is a desire to use the cultural to reposition or reframe the oppositional and dualistic relationship between human experience and theology as it has been played out in modern theology.

Practical Theology and Correlation

Practical theology has largely followed the pattern of discussion within modern theology. Many of its key theoretical frameworks have accepted the dualism inherent in the continuum, and it is this pattern that has framed practical theology. With an emphasis on practice and experience, practical theology has generally situated itself as a form of correlation, with positions being adopted that roughly correspond to those in the continuum. Correlation operates at a number of levels within practical theology. At its most basic level practical theology explores the many ways that the relationship between the practice of ministry and theology might be understood but correlation has also shaped practical theology by situating it within the discussion of a variety of 'relations' that follow the modernist project. These include the relationship between theologies of revelation and human experience, the relationship between the social sciences and theology, and the

---

89 Greeve Davaney, S. (2001), 'Theology and the Turn to Cultural Analysis', in Brown, D., Greeve Davaney, S. and Tanner, K. (2001), *Converging on Culture; Theologians in Dialogue with Cultural Analysis and Criticism*, Oxford: AAR/Oxford University Press, p. 9.

90 Greeve Davaney, 'Theology', p. 9.

91 Quoted in Greeve Davaney, 'Theology', p. 10.

way empirical methodologies, both quantitative and qualitative, might relate to systematic or doctrinal theology. How practical theology has been shaped by questions of relation and correlation and how it has started to shift towards the cultural can be illustrated from the work of three of the key contemporary figures in the field: Don Browning, Johannes van der Ven and Elaine Graham.

Don Browning has been highly influential in the development of practical theology. He constructs his method of practical theology by making use of Tracy's revised model of critical correlation.[92] His use of the revised model 'critically correlates' questions and answers from both theology, the Christian faith and questions and answers from the wider culture.[93] This approach is a revision of Tillich, because for Tillich, while correlation is also related to questions and answers, the questions are seen as emerging solely from the wider culture and are then answered in what Tillich calls the 'circle of Christian theology'.[94] In Browning's method the relationship between culture and theology is more dialogical and complex. He argues that the revised correlational method

> envisions theology as a mutually critical dialogue between interpre-
> tations of the Christian message and interpretations of contemporary
> cultural experiences and practices. Stated more explicitly, Christian
> theology becomes a critical dialogue between the implicit questions
> and the explicit answers of the Christian classics and the explicit
> questions and the implicit answers of contemporary cultural experi-
> ences and practices. According to [this approach], the Christian
> theologian must in principle have this critical conversation with 'all
> other answers' from wherever they come.[95]

---

92 Browning, D. (1991), *A Fundamental Practical Theology: Descriptive and Strate-gic Proposal*, Minneapolis: Fortress Press; see also Browning, D. (2000), 'Pastoral Theol-ogy in a Puralistic Age', in Woodward, J. and Pattison, S. (eds) (2000), *The Blackwell Reader in Pastoral and Practical Theology*, Oxford: Blackwell p. 93.

93 Browning, 'Pastoral', p. 93.

94 Tillich, P. (1951), *Systematic Theology*, vol. 1, Chicago: University of Chicago Press, p. 8.

95 Browning, quoted in Lynch, G. (2005), *Understanding Theology and Popular Cul-ture*, Oxford: Blackwell, p. 103.

Browning represents a liberal Protestant tradition in practical theology. Johannes van der Ven in contrast is a Catholic practical theologian who approaches the question of relation and correlation by developing what he calls 'empirical theology'. While he draws upon very different theological sources to Browning, van der Ven replicates the modernist separation of experience and theology. He traces what he sees as a narrative of relationship between theology and experience as 'monodisciplinarity, multi-disciplinarity, inter-disciplinarity, and intra-disciplinarity'.[96] Mono-disciplinarity he likens to forms of applied theology where principles are worked out through systematic or biblical studies and then applied to practice. Multi-disciplinarity utilizes the methods and perspectives of the social sciences and then reflects on these theologically. Inter-disciplinarity is similar to multi-disciplinarity but it is more akin to Browning in that a dialogue is established between the areas of thought. Van der Ven's preference is for his fourth model. 'The intra-disciplinary model requires that theology itself become empirical, that is that it expands its traditional range of instruments, consisting of literary-historical and systematic methods and techniques, in the direction of empirical methodology.'[97] Van der Ven's suggestion is that theology might adopt empirical methodologies from the social sciences and utilize these in the service of a theological frame. He sets up the relationship by arguing that, 'The direct object of empirical theology therefore is the faith and practice of the people concerned. The social sciences are used to further this enterprise and theology is dependent upon these disciplines within practical theology.'[98]

Empirical theology and the revised method of correlation represent two of the key streams of thought in practical theology. They develop different methodologies but they are both centred around the key issue of the problem of relationship between theory and practice, theology and experience, and the social sciences and systematic theology. The problematizing of relations and the advocacy of correlation or intra-disciplinarity serves to illustrate how these forms of practical theology echo the key concerns of the wider theological conversation. They

96 Van der Ven, J. (1990), *Practical theology and Empirical Approach*, trans. Schultz, B., Kampen: Peeters, pp. 89ff.

97 Van der Ven, *Practical*, p. 100.

98 Van der Ven, *Practical*, p. 100.

share the central problematic of the relationship between theology and human experience in modernity. Their methods clearly show more than a passing resemblance to those types of theology that are located around the mid-point in Ford's continuum.

If Browning and van der Ven situate practical theology within a recognizable modern conversation in theology, Elaine Graham's work is significant because it seeks to move the discipline beyond the question of relations. Central to this project is her use of culture as a theological category. Graham is concerned to relocate pastoral or practical theology within what she calls 'postmodern perspectives'.[99] She does this by drawing upon gender theory to argue for the truth-claims which are located in the '*practical wisdom* of the faithful practising community'.[100] She is critical of Browning's emphasis upon practical theology as the production of ethical perspectives derived from the practice of communities. Rather she seeks to interpret the contingent and performative nature of theology located in the practices of communities.[101] 'Pastoral theology is an interpretative discipline enabling faith-communities to give a public and critical account of their performative truth-claims. It attempts to capture glimpses of Divine activity amidst human practice.'[102]

The Convergence on Culture

For the ministerial practitioner practical theology holds a great deal of promise. It is the one area of theology that intentionally sets out to help the minister to wrestle with questions that come out of practice and church life. But practical theology can be experienced as frustrating. Practitioners come to theological education habituated to express faith and reason from within an embodied faith. It is practical theology that tends to socialize the practitioner into a fragmented and atomized take on the theological task.

---

99 Graham, E. (1996), *Transforming Practice: Pastoral Theology in an Age of Uncertainty*, London: Mowbray, p. 3.

100 Graham, *Transforming*, p. 140.

101 Graham, E. 'practical theology as Transforming Practice', in Woodward and Pattison, *Blackwell*, p. 113.

102 Graham, 'Practical', p. 113.

At heart this fragmentation comes from the way that practical theology has been shaped by the central problematic within modern theology. As they participate in their theological education ministers are socialized into viewing the theological task through the various dualisms that have shaped the pattern of debate within modern theology. The corelational approach of Browning and the intra-disciplinary method of van der Ven share the pattern of relations that is seen in the typologies presented by Ford, Tracy and others. In van der Ven's empirical theology the central problematic is set up between academic disciplines. So to be successful in doing empirical theology a method must be established to reconcile social science and theology. In Browning's revised correlational method the problematic rests on the relationship between human experience more generally and theology.

In practical theology and in systematic or doctrinal theology there has been a convergence around culture and the cultural. One of the reasons for this is the sense that culture as a category offers the promise of a theology that is not determined by a problematic based on the dualistic reading of experience and doctrine. In systematic theology this cultural turn is seen in the work of people such as George Lindbeck and more recently Kathryn Tanner. In practical theology a similar shift towards culture theology is seen in Elaine Graham's work. For Tanner and for Graham the cultural suggests a move beyond the modern paradigm towards a 'postmodern' theology. The implication is not simply that this represents the development of a type among other types of modern theology. The turn to culture is a 'post' precisely because it is seen as a discontinuity with the modern patterning of theology as it is framed within the continuum. For practical theology this 'post' is particularly significant because it addresses the problems associated with the fragmentation and atomization within theological education and therefore goes some way towards helping the ministerial practitioner to find a more sympathetic form of theological reasoning and reflection on practice.

The move towards culture as a key category in systematic and practical theology is a positive move because it means that theologians are tending to see 'ideas' about God as somehow connected and conditioned by historical and social realities. So disembodied theology is gradually being replaced by a concern to locate the doctrinal in the practices and expression of Christian communities and traditions. This shift towards the embodied is a welcome development for the puzzled practitioner, because it leads to a more hospitable and friendly form of theologizing. Doctrine that is read within the context of the life of the Church is obviously much more familiar territory for the minister. As a result the divide between thinking academically and thinking as a ministerial professional is effectively collapsed. So the kind of critique, analysis, theological construction and creativity demanded by academic work can no longer be seen as being a different kind of thinking to that which takes place on a day-to-day basis in Christian communities. When ministers preach sermons, design liturgies, choose hymns, make pastoral decisions, plan programmes of mission, and so on, they are already participating in the expression and circulation of theology. This kind of thinking is not different in essence from academic reasoning. Similarly when church members take part in study groups, listen to a teaching session at a Christian festival or read a book they find in the local Christian bookstore, they are engaging in activities that form a continuity with academic work. The difference between these forms of practical thinking and the practice of academic reasoning has more to do with focus and attention rather than with any disciplinary boundary.

Moreover, as a consequence of the emphasis upon culture it is no longer credible for the minister, or indeed the theologian, to suggest that they are able to step outside the situation to view the Church or its expression. The assumption that it is necessary to adopt a distanced and supposedly 'objective' perspective to think theologically is therefore increasingly seen as a questionable consequence of modernist dualism. This has implications for practical theology, which has tended to reinforce the dislocation between lived traditions and theological reflection through interpretative patterns such as the pastoral cycle. If theological reasoning forms a continuity with the kind of thinking already taking place in Christian communities then it is no longer sustainable to encourage practitioners that there should be such a thing as a distinct moment called 'theological reflection'. If we accept the contingency of the cultural then this means that theology and theologizing of all kinds takes place within and reflects the interests and commitments of individuals and communities. Academic practice therefore cannot be seen as a privileged, distinct or objective place.

Theology that is done in relation to the lived reality of the Church requires a familiarity with the life and expression of the Christian community. This is more good news for the minister who is going through theological education. The turn to the cultural means that academics must increasingly be orientated towards the lived experience of faith. So the minister and the academic are much more likely to find that they are meeting on common ground. In fact the emphasis on the particular and the lived means that the theological and cultural capital that the practitioner brings to the academic process is increasingly valued. Ministers are actively participating in the life of the Church in ways that most academics find hard to sustain, and they inevitably know more about their own communities than even the best-informed teacher.

So a practical theology that foregrounds the cultural has the potential to transform the way that ministers are educated. The tensions and problems that many practitioners experience as they go through their training are addressed by the new emphasis on the lived and the embodied. Having said this, while there has been a convergence on culture in practical theology and in systematic theology, it is striking that despite this interest there has so far not been an extended discussion of cultural studies as a possible dialogue partner in this enterprise.[103] My

---

103 A number of recent theological works have dealt directly with the relationship between theology and culture. None of these discuss cultural studies in any depth. Tanner, K. (1997), *Theories of Culture: A New Agenda for Theology*, Minneapolis: Fortress, is one of the key monographs, which explores the significance of contemporary theories of culture for theology. Her work has put the cultural on the agenda for theology. Her treatment of culture, however, largely ignores the area of cultural studies, resting mainly on an examination of ideas of culture within anthropology. Ward, G. (2005), *Cultural Transformation and Religious Practice*, Cambridge: Cambridge University Press, deals with the cultural primarily as cultural theory and thus locates it within philosophical territory. Gorringe, T. (2004), *Furthering Humanity: A Theology of Culture*, Aldershot: Ashgate, develops his theory in relation to notions of high culture/low culture and the early theories of Raymond Williams and Stuart Hall. He uses the idea of folk culture and a liberationist theology to pursue a critique of the 'culture industry' and popular media-generated culture. Lynch, G. (2005), *Understanding Theology and Popular Culture*, Oxford: Blackwell, is designed as an introductory text in this area and surveys key theories in contemporary cultural studies. It relies on existing patterns of linking culture and theology as correlation drawn from Tracy via Don Browning. Cobb, K. (2005), *The Blackwell Guide to Theology and Popular Culture*, Oxford: Blackwell, rests very heavily on Tillich. He reads popular culture as text, developing a depth analysis based on notions of ultimate concern.

own journey in ministry with young people has led me to value cultural studies as a major resource for theological work. Cultural studies helped me to understand the media-related popular space that I shared with the young people I had got to know, but these cultural insights were framed within a theological perspective that I found in mission studies, and this will be the focus of the next chapter.

2

Missiology and Culture

Mission studies has long ceased to be just for missionaries working 'overseas'. Increasingly we see mission as central to every kind of ministry. As a youth worker it took a while for me to realize that a discussion of the use of the coconut in Polynesian worship might be of significance to my work with Goth bands in England, or that the problems that Vincent Donovan found as he tried to share faith by telling Bible stories in Africa to the Masai would be similar to the problems that I was facing.[104] Yet these accounts of the expression of faith, in quite different parts of the world, gave me a crucial insight into the importance of contextualization for my own work. It wasn't that these examples of mission told me what to do. Rather they helped me to see the extent to which my own understanding of faith and the Church, of which I was a part, were shaped by a particular cultural setting.

In recent years the relationship between culture and the Church has become one of the most pressing issues in Western church life. As the Anglican *Mission Shaped Church* report argues, the Church stands before a 'significant opportunity' because 'Western society has undergone a massive transition in recent decades.'[105] The report makes a direct link between Church and mission. The Anglican Church, it says, is called to minister to the nation as a whole and if the Church is to minister to a society that is undergoing rapid and fundamental change then it too must expect to change. This argument is heavily influenced by an approach to faith and its expression that is derived from mission studies.

---

104 Amannaki Havea, S. (1987), *South Pacific Theology*, Oxford: Regnum Books; Donovan, V. (1978), *Christianity Rediscovered: An Epistle From the Masai*, London: SCM Press.

105 Archbishops' Council, *Mission*, p. 1.

For the practitioner the academic distinction between missiology and practical theology has become rather blurred. Mission has tended to merge with ministry as churches have responded to the increasing cultural exchange and diversity caused by globalization and migration. At the same time, mission organizations have refocused their work and expertise to reflect the new pluralism, and 'mission studies' has been repositioned as a vital resource for church life wherever that life is located. More recently the new ecclesiology associated with the Emerging Church and Fresh Expressions has grown from questions of culture and cultural change. This interest in culture in the Western Church has led to a renewed engagement with missiology. At the same time in practical theology the rise in interest in the expression of religious communities and in the various forms of liberation theology has also tended to locate the discussion of the relationship between theology and practice within the questions related to context and contextualization. This interest in context and culture has meant that practical theology has shifted its focus towards areas more traditionally associated with missiology.

Missiology, however, is of particular interest because it has been the area of theological work that has most consistently focused on the question of faith as it is expressed within and across cultures. Since the early 1950s mission studies has developed as a multi-disciplinary field of study concerned with the transmission of faith. Although theology has remained as a key frame of reference, missiologists have utilized a wide range of social-scientific methods of enquiry, particularly those found within anthropology.[106] As a consequence a nuanced and long-standing theological discourse has arisen within the study of mission related to questions of culture. How faith can be expressed within and between 'cultures' has been variously described as indigenization,[107] translation,[108] contextualization,[109] transformation,[110]

---

106 Luzbetak, L. J. (1988), *The Church and Cultures: New Perspectives in Missiological Anthropology*, Maryknoll: Orbis, p. 14.

107 Kraft, C. H. and Wisley, T. (eds.) (1979), *Readings in Dynamic Indigeneity*, Pasadena: William Carey Library.

108 Sanneh, L. (1991), *Translating the Message: The Missionary Impact on Culture*, Maryknoll: Orbis.

109 Bevans, S. (2002), *Models of Contextual Theology* (2nd edn), Maryknoll: Orbis.

110 Samuel, V. and Sugden, C. (eds) (1999), *Mission as Transformation: A Theology of the Whole Gospel*, Oxford: Regnum Books.

inculturation[111] and local, praxis or liberation theology.[112] What these terms have in common is that they represent a vigorous engagement with questions of theology and culture. Within missiology, however, there is no common ground on what is meant by culture or indeed what is meant by 'theology'. Like practical theology, however, mission studies has been affected by, and forms a part of, the conversation within theology concerning modernity. So mission studies, like practical theology, has tended to frame its approach to the translation of faith through the dualistic patterns in modern theology.

Christ and Culture

Although it is not strictly mission studies, Richard Niebuhr's *Christ and Culture*[113] has exercised a significant influence within missiology. Niebuhr shares the way of seeing in modern theology represented by the continuum. So he structures the relationship between culture and theology through a series of types or positions. At one end of the continuum he places what he calls the 'Christ against culture' position and at the other the 'Christ of culture' position. These responses to culture form the poles in his version of the continuum. The Christ against culture position, says Niebuhr, is reflected in those who see the gospel primarily as oppositional. According to this position, 'Whatever may be the customs of the society in which the Christian lives, and whatever the human achievements it conserves, Christ is seen as opposed to them, so that he confronts men with a challenge of an "either–or" decision.'[114] The Christ of culture position argues that in Jesus there is seen the fulfilment of human aspirations and values.[115] Thus in this position there is a direct identification between cultural life and Christian expression and so Christ forms part of the cultural heritage – what is to be conserved and what is to be transmitted – across generations.[116]

---

111 Shorter, A. (1988), *Toward a Theology of Inculturation*, London: Geoffrey Chapman.

112 Schreiter, R. J. (1985), *Constructing Local Theologies*, London: SCM Press.

113 Niebuhr, R. H. (1951), *Christ and Culture*, New York: Harper & Row.

114 Niebuhr, *Christ*, p. 40.

115 Niebuhr, *Christ*, p. 40.

116 Niebuhr, *Christ*, p. 41.

Between these two poles are clustered three approaches to Christ and culture, which in various ways develop strategies to combine or take account of opposition or accommodation. These he calls Christ above culture, Christ and culture in paradox and Christ the transformer of culture positions.

The influence of Niebuhr's treatment of the issue of gospel and culture in mission studies can be seen in Stephen Bevans's work on contextual theology.[117] In *Models of Contextual Theology* Bevans develops a continuum based on six models: the anthropological model, the praxis model, the synthetic model, the translation model and the countercultural model. He places these models on a continuum where at one extreme there is an emphasis on human experience, culture and location, and at the other extreme there is a contrasting emphasis on scripture and tradition. Thus in his typology what he calls 'the anthropological model' emphasizes the importance of culture and identity to the theological enterprise. The fulfilment of the human person and their potential is central to this approach to contextual theology.[118]

> This model centers on the value and goodness of *anthropos*, the human person. Human experience, as it is limited and yet realized in culture, social change, and geographical and historical circumstances, is considered the basic criterion of judgement as to whether a particular contextual expression is genuine or not.[119]

The translation model emphasizes tradition and scripture in what has become known as the 'kernel and husk' approach to contextualization. Here the Christian faith is represented as an unchanging essence or kernel, which must be translated into the language and cultural expression of a community.[120] The praxis model is identified with the various liberation theologies but it also includes patterns of theology that emphasize practice and action in theological expression. For Bevans, 'the key presupposition of the praxis model is the insight that the highest level of knowing is intelligent and responsible doing'.[121] The

---

117 Bevans, *Models*.
118 Bevans, *Models*, p. 54.
119 Bevans, *Models*, p. 55.
120 Bevans, *Models*, pp. 37ff.
121 Bevans, *Models*, p. 73.

synthetic model is closely related to the methods of correlation in other typologies, in that it is situated at the mid-point along the continuum. The model attempts to develop a synthesis between contexts and theological expression. It also looks beyond a particular cultural context to wider patterns across cultures.[122] The transcendent model attempts to develop contextual theology from transcendent categories of what it means to be human or spiritual. The starting point is not tradition or context, rather it is 'transcendental, concerned with one's own religious experience and one's own experience of oneself'.[123]

In the first edition of *Models of Theology* Bevans followed the standard five types, as they are used by Frei, Tracy and Ford, in developing his continuum. At one extreme he placed the anthropological model and at the other the translation model. In the second edition however he added at the one extreme a sixth model: this he called 'the countercultural model'. This model, which he developed through dialogue with the Lesslie Newbigin-inspired 'Gospel and our culture' movement in the USA, places a much greater emphasis upon maintaining a theological identity in relation to culture.[124] What emerges in this model, says Bevans, is an approach to theological work, which recognizes the significance of cultural and social relations while it also places a commitment to the gospel as the core value in relation to this context. 'Contextual theology is best done, they say by an analysis of context and by respect for it, but by allowing the gospel to take the lead in the process so that the context is shaped and formed by the reality of the gospel and not vice-versa.'[125]

Bevans's presentation of mission theology as a series of related models therefore reproduces the characteristic features of modern theology as they are presented within the interpretative device of a continuum. His work illustrates the extent to which mission studies, like practical theology, has been influenced by the gravitational pull within modern theology. This has meant that missiology has tended to deal with the cultural through the lens of the problematic of relations. Thus culture within this framework is situated at the extreme or the pole that

---

122 Bevans, *Models*, pp. 89–90.
123 Bevans, *Models*, p. 104.
124 Bevans, *Models*, p. xvi.
125 Bevans, *Models*, p. 119.

corresponds to the experiential/expressivist. Yet as culture has become more central to theological discussion, mission studies has tended to stress the centrality of 'context' in all kinds of theology. So Bevans argues that a consideration of context is a 'theological imperative'. This imperative means that theology must always be qualified. 'There is no such thing as "theology"; there is only *contextual* theology: *feminist* theology, *black* theology, *Filipino* theology, *Asian-American* theology, *African* theology and so forth.'[126] Doing theology contextually, says Bevans, is not an option, rather it is an inevitability. For Niebuhr, Christ and culture operate in separate but related spheres. Bevans's assertion that all theology is 'cultural' challenges this distinction and yet paradoxically his typology tends to reproduce the framework that Niebuhr shares with modern theology. Yet as the understanding of culture has developed, similar changes to those seen in practical theology and systematic theology are also evident in mission studies. Central to this change has been a slowly developing consensus around culture as a key factor in all forms of theological expression. In the first instance this acceptance of the cultural develops from mission practice where Westerners seek to communicate faith across cultures, but very soon the insights gained in non-Western contexts are seen as being crucial to mission wherever it takes place. This is why mission studies has been at the heart of calls for new expressions of Church in the UK and the USA and why youth workers, and others who seek to minister beyond the familiar Church culture, have seen missiology as the key theological discipline that speaks to their endeavours.

Culture in Mission Studies

The view that theology is always related to questions of contextualization and culture is widely held by missiologists. Andrew Kirk argues that theology does not exist without mission. All theology, he says, is based on some notion of a connection to wider social and cultural issues, and even when it claims to be 'non-partisan, [it] is in reality thoroughly committed'.[127] Not only is theology missiological by its very

---

126 Bevans, *Models*, p. 3.

127 Kirk, A. (1999), *What is Mission? Theological Explorations*, London: DLT, p. 11.

nature but, says Kirk, the gospel is always 'mediated' within culture.[128] Andrew Walls suggests that there is an indigenizing principle in Christian theology. At root, he says, indigenization comes from the way that God accepts us as we are. This includes the cultural and social expression of life. Indigenization means that faith is expressed within culture and takes its forms. All churches are 'culture churches, including our own', says Walls.[129] At the same time there is a parallel and opposing principle, which he calls the pilgrim principle. This principle arises from the fact that while God takes people as they are, God also transforms and changes them.[130] The translation of the gospel therefore has these two aspects: expression within culture, and the conversion or transformation of that culture. Not all missiologists would argue that theology is in some way subsumed in contextualization, yet most argue that there is a vital link between the expression of faith and issues of culture.

In Roman Catholic theology there has been a growing acknowledgement since Vatican II, and particularly in *Evangelii Nuntiandi*,[131] that the expression of the faith implies the evangelization of all cultures: those of the first world as well as those of the third world.[132] Catholic missiologists have generally adopted the term 'inculturation' for this relationship between faith and culture. With its origins in the anthropological term 'enculturation', the word was first used by Masson in 1962 and gained popularity among the Jesuits.[133] Inculturation, says Aylward Shorter, is not simply concerned with the moments when the faith is first expressed within culture. Rather inculturation should been seen as an ongoing process in culture.[134]

Evangelical mission theology has generally related more strongly to notions of translation or contextualization. Through the work of

---

128 Kirk, *What*, p. 75.

129 Walls, A. (1996), *The Missionary Movement in Christian History: Studies in the Transmission of Faith*, Edinburgh: T & T Clark, pp. 7–8.

130 Walls, *Missionary*, p. 8.

131 Paul VI, (1975), *Evangelii Nuntiandi*, Vatican: Sacred Congregation for Evangelization.

132 Arbuckle, G. (1990), *Earthing the Gospel: An Inculturation Handbook for Pastoral Workers*, London: Geoffrey Chapman, p. 16.

133 Bosch, D. (1992), *Transforming Mission: Paradigm Shifts in Theology of Mission*, Maryknoll: Orbis, p. 446.

134 Shorter, *Toward*, p. 11.

Eugene Nida and Charles Kraft ideas of dynamic equivalence translation or indigenization have been widely adopted by evangelicals.[135]
Both Nida and Kraft developed their understanding of cross-cultural
mission through a multi-disciplinary approach derived primarily from
anthropology. These evangelical theories of contextualization tend to
emphasize the way that the biblical message of the gospel is translated from one context to another context. Roman Catholic notions
of inculturation on the other hand tend to be focused on the way that
the Christian Church and its tradition and practices find cultural expression across cultures. The term contextualization has tended to be
most closely associated with theologies of liberation. Robert Schreiter,
however, identifies two different forms of contextual theologies. The
first of these focus on cultural identity, and these he calls 'ethnographic
theologies'. The second concentrates on 'oppression and social ills',
and these are the liberation theologies.[136] Contextualizing theologies
are different from what he calls 'adaption' approaches to theologizing
because they develop a 'local theology', which 'begins with the needs
of a people in a concrete place, and from there moves to traditions of
faith'.[137]

From this brief discussion it is clear that contextual theologies,
whatever their particular emphasis, all deal in one way or another with
issues of culture. The claim that all theology is missional or contextual
is more contentious. What seems clear, however, is that both the Roman
Catholic inculturation and the evangelical translation are based on the
notion that there is a space where the Church or theologians can operate that is outside of the cultural. It is precisely this space which Bevans
attacks when he argues that theology as an 'objective science' is no
longer plausible. In place of this claim for a separate and privileged
place beyond the cultural, Bevans argues that theology is of necessity
contextual, and he therefore embraces the cultural and the situated.[138]
While some theologians may want to temper these claims somewhat,
what is clear is that there is a convergence on culture in mission studies

---

135 Nida, E. (1954), *Customs, Culture and Christianity*, London: Tyndale Press;
Kraft, C. H. (1984), *Anthropology for Christian Witness*, Maryknoll: Orbis.
136 Schreiter, *Constructing*, p. 13.
137 Schreiter, *Constructing*, p. 13.
138 Bevans, *Models*, p. 4.

that parallels developments in practical theology and in modern theology more generally.

Cross-Cultural Mission Relativizes Western Theology

The emphasis on culture and its relation to theology is particularly significant for the current turn to culture in Western theology. For the ministerial professional who is engaged in the expression of faith in the Emerging Church, or among young people, or within migrant communities, mission studies as a conversation around culture and theology is a vital resource, not least because it is in cross-cultural mission that our own cultural, ecclesial and theological norms are seen to be relativized. It has been common, says Lamin Sanneh, for Western missionaries engaged in cross-cultural communication to experience a sense of dislocation from their own culture. This dislocation often leads them to question their own cultural and theological assumptions. For Sanneh it is in cross-cultural mission that 'A fresh standard of discernment is introduced by which the essence of the gospel is unscrambled from one cultural yoke in order to take firm hold in a different culture.'[139] Against the prevailing wisdom, argues Sanneh, Western mission often led not so much to a critical judgement on non-Western cultures as to a critique of the culture and theology of the missionaries themselves.[140] Charles Kraft makes a very similar observation when he remarks that the experience of many missionaries is one of frustration and confusion when they realize that 'the theology taught to us in our home churches, Bible schools, Christian colleges, and seminaries turns out to be extremely difficult to use in cross-cultural contexts *in the form in which we learned it*'.[141] This means, says Kraft, that cross-cultural mission requires that missionaries must take a risk with their own theological frameworks in order that they may learn to communicate faith.[142]

The relativizing of Western culture and theology experienced by Western missionaries has led missiologists to frame their understanding

---

139 Sanneh, *Translating*, p. 25.
140 Sanneh, *Translating*, p. 25.
141 Kraft, *Christianity*, p. 13.
142 Kraft, *Christianity*, p. 19.

of theology within a pluralist framework. This pluralism extends not simply across contemporary cultural divides, it has also led to the widespread reading of Christian history and historical theology as a series of differing cultural paradigms. A number of contemporary missiologists have sought to understand the relationship between theology and cultural pluralism through the lens of distinct historical periods or paradigm shifts.[143] It is David Bosch's *Transforming Mission* which sets out this theory in the most detail. Bosch bases his reading of Christian mission as a series of paradigms on Hans Kung's periodization of Christian theology.[144] Kung's theory in turn rests on Thomas Kuhn's theory of the development of science through a series of revolutions or paradigm shifts.[145] The notion of a paradigm rests on the assertion that within each period Christians expressed and debated the faith within a set framework of understanding. The idea of paradigm shifts grows from the assertion that between one period or paradigm and the next Christians 'understood and experienced their faith in ways only partially commensurable with the understanding of believers of other eras'.[146] Bosch accepts that there are problems with the theory of paradigms, particularly as they relate to Christian theology. For instance, paradigms appear to overlap and live on in ecclesial life, and paradigms may also seem to be rediscovered in theology.[147] So he sets out to use the term as what he calls a 'working hypothesis'.[148] Bosch divides the history of mission into six paradigms: primitive Christianity; the patristic period; the Middle Ages; the Reformation; the Enlightenment; and the ecumenical era.[149] Bosch's theory of paradigm shifts in mission has been critiqued, for instance, in that it fails to do justice to third-world history and theology, indigenous spiritualities, ecology and pneumatology, and that it is not adequately based in empirical frameworks.[150] Despite these failings *Transforming Mission* has been

---

143 See Walls, *Missionary*, pp. 3ff., and also Sanneh, *Translation*, p. 6.
144 Bosch, *Transforming*, pp. 181–2.
145 Bosch, *Transforming*, p. 182.
146 Bosch, *Transforming*, p. 183.
147 Bosch, *Transforming*, p. 186.
148 Bosch, *Transforming*, p. 184.
149 Bosch, *Transforming*, p. 188.
150 See Verstraelen, F. J. (1996), 'Africa in David Bosch's Missiology: Survey and Proposal', in Saayman, W. and Kritzinger, K. (eds) (1996), *Mission in Bold Humility: David*

among the primary texts in missiology since its publication.[151] Its significance is that it has added a historical force of relativization to the contemporary cultural experience of missionaries.

Transforming Mission was seminal in that it suggested that there was a renewed significance in the notion that faith, ecclesial life, mission and theology have shifted with cultural change across generations. This insight in and of itself is perhaps not particularly acute or original. Its force has been felt in the way that it combines two factors. The first is the argument that we are currently in the middle of a sixth paradigm shift from the Enlightenment paradigm to an emerging ecumenical paradigm. The second is the link which is made between this assertion and the experience of a missiological engagement with culture. It is this assertion, combined with a concern for a missional approach to a changing Western culture, which was taken up and championed by Lesslie Newbigin. Newbigin is significant because his writing articulates the thinking in missiology to the wider developments in modern theology.

Mission to Western Culture

During the 1980s the missionary bishop and ecumenical theologian Lesslie Newbigin set out in a series of books and articles an argument for mission to Western culture. Growing originally out of work with the World Council of Churches, he published under their auspices *The Other Side of 1984*.[152] This led eventually to the launch of the 'Gospel and Culture' programme.[153] Newbigin takes insights from missiology and uses them to address what he calls 'modern western culture'.[154] In particular he identifies the way that contemporary missionaries have experienced a weakening of confidence in their own inherited

---

Bosch's Work Considered, Maryknoll: Orbis, p. 12; Kim, K. (2000), 'Post-modern Mission a Paradigm Shift in David Bosch's Theology of Mission?', in Yates, T. (ed.), *Mission – and Invitation to God's Future*, Sheffield: Cliff College, pp. 99–102.

151 Kim, 'Post-modern', p. 1.

152 Newbigin, L. (1983), *The Other Side of 1984: Questions for the Churches*, Geneva: World Council of Churches.

153 Weston, P. (ed.) (2006), *Lesslie Newbigin Missionary Theologian: A Reader*, London: SPCK, p. 13.

154 Newbigin, L. (1989), *The Gospel in a Pluralist Society*, London: SPCK, p. 1.

expressions of the faith. As a result, says Newbigin, they have become aware of the extent to which in their sharing of faith they have 'often confused culturally conditioned perceptions with the substance of the gospel'.[155] He embraces the idea of contextualization within missiology yet he is critical of the way that the literature in mission studies has failed to deal with the culture from which this work is generated, namely, modern Western culture.[156]

Newbigin follows the anthropological understanding of culture adopted by early missiology. Culture, he says, is, 'the sum total of ways of living developed by a group of human beings and handed on from generation to generation'.[157] He sees language as central to the notion of culture, and around this centre, he says, there are grouped artistic, technological and political ways of organizing. Crucially he argues that fundamental to culture are beliefs, experiences and practices 'that seek to grasp and express the ultimate nature of things'.[158] These together act to give meaning to life and they claim a 'final loyalty'. This latter area Newbigin identifies as the place of religion in culture.[159] For Newbigin the gospel is shaped by the life, ministry, death and resurrection of Jesus Christ. This gospel is always expressed in culture, and like Walls's idea of the pilgrim principle, it also calls into question every human culture.[160] From here a model for the communication of the gospel is developed. First the gospel must be shared in the thought forms of the culture within which it is communicated, but second, as it is communicated it should also offer a critique of that culture.[161]

From this starting point Newbigin sets out to address what he sees as the 'syncretism' in Western Christianity.[162] He uses Berger's theory of secularization and plausibility structures to argue that the Western Church has imported an alien understanding of faith as relating to the private and personal spheres. This, he says, is the 'operative plausibility

155 Newbigin, *Gospel*, p. 2.
156 Newbigin, *Gospel*, p. 3.
157 Newbigin, *Gospel*, p. 3.
158 Newbigin, *Gospel*, p. 3.
159 Newbigin, *Gospel*, p. 3.
160 Newbigin, *Gospel*, p. 4.
161 Newbigin, *Gospel*, pp. 5–6.
162 Newbigin, *Gospel*, p. 9.

structure of the modern world'.[163] He makes the link between this plausibility structure and what he terms the dominant Western scientific worldview.[164] He traces the roots between this worldview and the effects of the Enlightenment, in particular Kantian metaphysics.[165] While he deals with these developments primarily in terms of the history of ideas, he makes the point that these ideas function as a way of life:

> [P]lainly what we call Western culture is much more than a body of ideas. It is a whole way of organizing human life that both rests on and in turn supports and validates the ideas …[166]

Newbigin argues that the project of liberal theology in the nineteenth and twentieth centuries has developed in response to the dominant enlightenment understanding of the relationship between faith and knowledge.[167] It is this move which he identifies as syncretistic. In short he launches an assault on these developments in the Western Church, which he regards as being an abandonment of the public nature of belief, and in response he argues that the gospel itself offers an alternative plausibility structure. It is not possible, he says, to argue rationally for this position, rather this is a matter of costly obedience and faithfulness on the part of Christian people.[168] The missionary approach to Western culture will 'call for radical conversion'.[169] 'This will be not only a conversion of the will and of the feelings but a conversion of the mind – a "paradigm shift" that leads to a new vision of how things are.'[170] The result will be the development of a new plausibility structure in which 'the most real of realities is the living God whose character is "rendered" for us in the pages of scripture'.[171]

Newbigin's significance does not lie so much in his critique of the

---

163 Newbigin, *Gospel*, p. 14.
164 Newbigin, *Gospel*, p. 15.
165 Newbigin, *Gospel*, p. 25.
166 Newbigin, *Gospel*, p. 29.
167 Newbigin, *Gospel*, p. 45.
168 Newbigin, *Gospel*, p. 64.
169 Newbigin, *Gospel*, p. 64.
170 Newbigin, *Gospel*, p. 64.
171 Newbigin, *Gospel*, p. 64.

Enlightenment roots of modern epistemology, rather it is to be found in his starting point that Western culture itself should be the context for a mission theology. He has been variously critiqued both for his assertion of a new paradigm for plausibility and also for his theological positivism.[172] Hunsberger makes the point that Newbigin's thinking should perhaps be situated as part of the growing debate concerning the postmodern, although Newbigin himself was not taken up with these ideas as such.[173] I want to develop this insight by reference to Newbigin's understanding of culture. While the direction of his work has tended to focus attention on philosophy, in his understanding of culture he starts by talking of a 'way of life' which is characteristic of societies, and this is centred on language. Around language lies the realm of the artistic, communication technologies and politics. Newbigin's strategy was to drive to the heart of these areas of expression through the notion of values. It is this move which Andrew Walker seeks to modify and correct.

In *Telling the Story* Walker builds on Newbigin's key assumptions. However, he develops these by a discussion of the place of technology, and the nature of consumption and the consumer, in this overall missiological framework. His work, Walker says, rests on two main assumptions. The first assumption is that 'Consumerism and mass communication are more influential in contemporary culture than academics in their universities or scientists in their laboratories.'[174] The second assumption is that: 'Modernity, the scientific-rationalist-industrial culture of the last 200 years, is not merely in advanced decay, but in the process of cultural transition.'[175] In the second of these assumptions Walker is not alone in missiological thinking. It is the first which is of particular significance. Walker's insight here is crucial to the understanding of contextualization and also to the

---

172 See Price, L. (2002), 'Churches and Postmodernity: Opportunity for Attitude Shift', in Foust, T. F., Hunsberger, G. R., Kirk, A. and Ustorf, W. (eds), *A Scandalous Prophet: The Way of Mission after Newbigin*, Grand Rapids: Eerdmans, p. 107.

173 Hunsberger, G. R. (2002), 'The Church in the Postmodern Transition', in Foust, T. F., Hunsberger, G. R., Kirk, A. and Ustorf, W. (eds), *A Scandalous Prophet: The Way of Mission after Newbigin*, Grand Rapids: Eerdmans.

174 Walker, A. (1996), *Telling the Story: Gospel Mission and Culture*, London: SPCK, p. xii.

175 Walker, *Telling*, p. xii.

development of a theory of the relationship between the 'way of seeing' represented by cultural studies and practical theology. He sets out to show how faith and technology have developed side by side in Western society. Technologies such as the telegraph, the radio and the television in the nineteenth and twentieth centuries are now supplemented by the impact of the new technologies of the internet and global communication. Walker makes a case for the significance of these forces in the shaping of church life. His argument is that mass communication and consumerism need to be at the heart of the debate concerning faith transmission. Consumer culture and the media ensured that the popular may be likened to the air that we all breathe or the water in the fish tank. We can't avoid being affected because we live in it and to some extent we need it to live. This realization has decisively shaped the contemporary debates concerning the Emerging Church and it has been at the heart of the growth in new forms of ministry, worship and mission. In this missiological context, cultural studies becomes a vital framework for developing an understanding of consumer culture. The next chapter explores how this field of study offers a way of seeing that might inform practical theology.

3

Doing Cultural Studies

Culture is a basic part of ministerial life. Ministers of all kinds are regularly called upon to move into unfamiliar cultural worlds. Clergy who are involved in chaplaincy, for instance, have to learn to minister in the 'cultural' context of a hospital or a prison. In the parish life, ministering to a family as they go through bereavement and helping them to prepare the funeral of a loved one can often demand a 'cultural' sensitivity and the ability to communicate across culture. Congregations are increasingly likely to be made up of people from a variety of backgrounds, and these multicultural Christian communities are themselves in turn seeking to minister in parishes shaped by ethnic, cultural and religious diversity. The relationship between ministry and culture is particularly apparent in youth work. Working with young people involves finding ways to cross not only generational but also cultural boundaries. Culture is therefore very much part of the everyday experience of the minister.

Culture may be part of our everyday life, but understanding culture is far from straightforward. Culture is complex, but it is also all-pervasive and nowhere is this more the case than in academic study, where the 'cultural' has become a key category in a wide range of disciplines. So cultural studies might best be described as a tendency within and across disciplines rather than simply as a discipline in its own right.[176] It forms part of a turn towards culture that is evident in the social sciences, literary criticism, history and the humanities in general.[177] For Toby Miller the cultural has become a '"master-trope" in

---

176 Miller, T. (ed.) (2001), *A Companion to Cultural Studies*, Oxford: Blackwell, p. 1.

177 Tanner, K. (1997), *Theories of Culture*, Minneapolis: Fortress Press, p. ix.

the humanities, blending and blurring textual analysis of popular culture with social theory, and focusing on the margins of power rather than reproducing established lines of force and authority'.[178] Cultural studies examines how culture is 'used' by marginal groups. It focuses attention on the way that subcultures through consumption produce 'social values and cultural languages'.[179] Mark Smith suggests that the study of culture allows for the development of what he calls a 'post-disciplinary approach'. This approach breaks away from the domain of strict academic disciplinarity and 'tramples across boundaries and synthesizes good ideas and useful research strategies whatever their location'.[180] What emerges from this perspective is an understanding of the study of culture as a collection of ways of seeing that have been adapted and adopted across a whole range of academic disciplines.

So the convergence on culture within systematic theology, missiology and practical theology is part of a much more general 'turn' across academic disciplines. This shift reorientates practical theology by making a move beyond questions that relate to correlation. For just as it lacks plausibility to deal with culture as somehow separate from Christ or Christian expression, so also cultural studies cannot be situated through some form of correlation as a separate 'discipline'. Instead what is required is a way of working theologically which recognizes theology's own cultural contingency and deals with the theological as culture and culture as theological. This is what is meant by cultural studies as a way of seeing.

Cultural Studies and Inter-disciplinarity

Raymond Williams famously notes in *Keywords* that culture is one of the two or three most complicated words in the English language.[181] He does not wish, by such an observation, to encourage the unravelling of this complexity, rather he sees in the evolution of the word and its range of meanings evidence of a necessary and vital debate.

---

178 Miller, *Companion*, p. 1.
179 Miller, *Companion*, p. 1.
180 Smith, M. J. (2000), *Culture, Reinventing the Social Sciences*, Milton Keynes: Open University Press, p. 2.
181 Williams, R. (1976), *Keywords*, London: Fontana, p. 76.

This is a debate not so much about the word itself but concerning the problems which its variation in usage indicates.[182] That the meaning of culture is complex and has undergone significant change is therefore seen by Williams as part of a wider map derived from changes in five key terms; industry, democracy, class, art and culture.[183] The shifts in meaning with these words, he says, 'bear witness to a general change in our characteristic thinking about our common life'.[184]

He identifies the early uses of culture as a noun of process relating to the 'tending *of* something' or cultivation.[185] Alongside this notion of cultivation he traces three main strands in the use of the term. First, the tending of natural growth is extended to the aesthetic, intellectual and spiritual development of people. Second, culture relates to a particular 'way of life' of a group or a people. Third, culture is used of the works and practices of artistic and intellectual life.[186] For Williams these three strands of use indicate a field of enquiry and debate rather than an attempt to clarify and separate meaning. Reflecting on the way that these connections have affected both the arts and the social sciences, in his later work *Culture*, Williams identifies what he terms a convergence of enquiry around these clustered meanings. 'Thus there is some practical convergence between i) the anthropological and sociological senses of culture as a distinct "whole way of life" within which a distinct "signifying system" is seen not only as essential but as essentially involved in all forms of social activity and ii) the more specialized if also more common use of culture as "artistic" and "intellectual activities".'[187]

Williams's notion of convergence lays the framework for cultural studies as an approach to the culture that crosses disciplinary boundaries. For Williams culture relates not just to the anthropological but also to art. So sociological themes are articulated with questions concerning art and literary criticism. These together are linked (as a system of signification) to power relations in society. Culture as a way of

---

182 Williams, *Keywords*, p. 81.
183 Williams, R. (1958), *Culture and Society 1780–1950*, Harmondsworth: Penguin, p. 13.
184 Williams, *Culture and Society*, p. 13.
185 Williams, *Keywords*, p. 81.
186 Williams, *Keywords*, p. 81.
187 Williams, R. (1981), *Culture*, London: Fontana, p. 13.

life focuses attention on the lived reality of the 'ordinary'. Yet there is also a connection to be made between a whole way of life and cultural texts. Thus Williams locates questions that revolve around the production and values of cultural and artistic artefacts within the ordinary and the lived and also as part of issues that relate to the political. Through this reading of convergence around culture Williams lays the foundation for cultural studies as a way of seeing that exploits the fruitful interactions that come from reading the lived as a system of signs and the material and artistic as part of ethnography.

Discipline and Practice

Williams's influential work led to the development of what Kathryn Tanner calls the 'interdisciplinary melange' of British and US cultural studies.[188] From Williams the practice of cultural studies involved the study of a number of allied themes or areas of interest. The continuing influence of these converging themes is clearly evident in Rojek's suggestion that the practice of the study of culture involves four interconnecting 'components' that together make up what he calls 'the sphere of cultural studies'.[189] These are 'the observation of culture (genre), the manufacture of culture (production), the exchange of culture (consumption) and the contestation of culture (cultural politics)'.[190]

Genre involves the examination of cultural form and content. Questions here concern the way that particular cultural expressions relate to identity and difference. So genre, says Rojek, might involve representation in Goth culture or how women's magazines attract readers,

---

188 Tanner, *Theories*, p. ix. An account of the history of cultural studies is fraught with problems not least because, as Chris Barker says, even those most closely associated with its development have often resisted 'institutional legitimation' (Barker, C. (2007), *Cultural Studies: Theory and Practice* (2nd edn), London: Sage, p. 6). So while it is possible to identify significant figures, publications that form what Chris Rojek calls 'moments' in cultural studies, it is widely acknowledged that the history of the discipline is problematic (Rojek, C. (2007), *Cultural Studies*, Cambridge: Polity Press, pp. 39ff.); for contrasting accounts of the origins of cultural studies see also McGuigan, J. (1992), *Cultural Populism*, London: Routledge; Morley, D. and Chen, H. (1996), *Stuart Hall: Critical Dialogues in Cultural Studies*, London: Routledge; and Barker, *Cultural*.

189 Rojek, *Cultural*, p. 12.
190 Rojek, *Cultural*, p. 10.

or the way that culinary cultures relate to social differences.[191] Production relates to the creation of cultural meaning and issues concerning the interests behind 'the presentation of cultural form and content'.[192] This involves the consideration of questions associated with the way that companies produce cultural meanings. For instance, what do Adidas, Pepsi and Brylcreem intend when they use someone like David Beckham to endorse their products, or how do multinationals make use of branding to ensure consumers remain loyal to particular products?[193] Consumption relates to the way that 'cultural meanings are assimilated by consumers'.[194] This results in questions concerning the way that consumers exchange cultural texts and the relationship between the signifying nature of products and the construction of identity, opposition and social difference.[195] Cultural politics considers the way that 'meaning is presented, resisted and opposed through the process of cultural exchange'.[196] Questions here confront issues of power, knowledge and values or the way that branding can be resisted or the different influences that particular groups exercise in relation to the media.[197]

Practical Theology and Key Themes in the Study of Culture

The convergence of interests identified by Williams is also evident in Chris Barker's more recent summary of key themes in cultural studies. These eight themes, says Barker, 'regulate cultural studies as a discursive formation or language game'.[198] Barker's themes introduce cultural studies as a way of seeing. These themes are a way of introducing cultural studies as a resource that can inform and shape practical theology.

---

191 Rojek, *Cultural*, p. 10.
192 Rojek, *Cultural*, p. 10.
193 Rojek, *Cultural*, p. 10.
194 Rojek, *Cultural*, p. 11.
195 Rojek, *Cultural*, p. 11.
196 Rojek, *Cultural*, p. 11.
197 Rojek, *Cultural*, p. 11.
198 Barker, *Cultural*, p. 7.

Theme 1   *Culture and Signifying Practices*

Culture is related to the idea of shared social meanings or the way that people 'make sense of the world'.[199] Meanings are 'generated through signs, most notably those of language'.[200] Language constitutes objects as part of a system of meaning. So the study of culture involves an exploration of 'how meaning is produced symbolically in language as a signifying system'.[201]

To be a part of a Christian community means that we share in a signifying system. Participation in faith involves developing a competency in how these symbols work. This can be as simple as knowing what to do during an act of worship. For those of us who have grown up in the Church, the way that the community behaves and communicates may appear 'natural'. We have been socialized within a tradition. Our awareness of the particularity of our own familiar form of faith expression may only become clear when we encounter a different kind of Christian worship. So the charismatic Christian attending a Catholic church for the first time will find it strange even though it is ostensibly the same faith. My own sense of the way that faith operated as a particular form of cultural expression came as I went to church with young people who had never been to church. Looking through their eyes it became to clear to me that that church as I knew it was a strange and bewildering world to them. They helped me to see the extent to which my own faith was 'cultural'. Barker's first theme identifies the way that culture – and I would argue that this includes the culture of the Christian community – is made up of shared meanings.

Shared meanings are related to a system of signs that operate as a language. This is familiar territory for Christians. We are well aware of the way that faith is communicated through the symbolic. Churches are full of signs from stained-glass windows to the font. Religious language is nothing if it is not symbolic. Church tradition is made up of particular configurations of these signs. So what it means to be a Baptist or a Greek Orthodox comes not simply from an association with a particular group of Christians but from a much deeper identification

---

199 Barker, *Cultural*, p. 7.
200 Barker, *Cultural*, p. 7.
201 Barker, *Cultural*, pp. 7–8.

with a tradition. We operate as Christians by sharing in our church's distinctive signifying system. Participation in a Christian tradition is not limited to understanding the meaning of signs and how they work as language. To be Christian means that we also internalize tradition. It shapes our sense of self in relation to a community. Sharing in tradition also means that we have some competency in expressing our faith as part of this signifying system.

The first move in adopting cultural studies as a way of seeing within practical theology involves an orientation towards how Christian communities participate in the production of their own distinctive traditions. The shared meanings of a distinctive Christian tradition come from doctrinal formulation and church history, but they are also found in objects, music, clothing, lifestyle, food, and so on. The cultural perspective encourages a practical theology that sees all of these aspects of Christian life and expression working as shared communication. This means that the popular and the everyday is read alongside and in relation to the doctrinal, as both form part of the shared meanings of a community.

Theme 2   Representation

Barker sees cultural studies as being in large part centred on a consideration of the way that meanings are socially constructed and represented to us and by us as a signifying system. This involves an exploration of the way that texts generate meaning. Cultural representations and meanings, says Barker, 'have a certain materiality'.[202]

This theme focuses attention on the relationship between texts, meaning and communities. Practical theology needs to develop ways of seeing that enable practitioners to read the interplay between the materiality of representation and the meanings that communities make in relation to texts. An example of this would be the way that a parish church represents so much more than bricks and mortar. Church buildings carry a wide range of meanings both for those within and those beyond the Christian community. A church can be seen as representing the worshipping community or a denomination. It might also be read as a symbol of a divine presence in a locality. Through

---

202 Barker, *Cultural*, p. 8.

the memory of weddings, baptisms and funerals, churches also represent more personal meanings. At the same time, as historic buildings, churches are often associated with a sense of heritage, and they are therefore visited and admired for their architecture and monuments. In all of these ways the material nature of a church building can be seen as representing different kinds of meanings. These meanings are not necessarily inherent in the building: they are made, or constructed, by people in relation to the church. In turn the building itself appears to carry these meanings and represents them to us.

Representation is material, but this does not mean that it is limited to material things such as buildings or objects. Theological ideas, for instance, are representations. At a very basic level, theology is representation in the way that it uses narrative, metaphor and analogy. These representations are also material. We represent the theological in prayers, sermons, debate, creeds and academic texts. Representation also relates to communities and individuals. Priests and ministers are figures that are generally regarded as meaningful, and the wider Christian community also functions as a symbol. Recognizing the complex interplay between communities, texts and meanings in representation is a key task for practical theology. There is a clear missiological imperative for this. We urgently need to find ways of seeing that enable practitioners to explore how representation works both within and beyond Christian communities, if we are to be able to formulate theological approaches to ministry or mission that are contextual and culturally relevant.

Theme 3   Materialist and Non-reductionist

The study of culture largely takes place, says Barker, in the context of modern industrialized economies. Representation is produced by companies that are seeking to make a profit. Cultural studies is therefore focused on the material in that it is 'concerned to explore how and why meanings are inscribed at the moment of production'.[203] These issues relate to questions of power and the distribution of economic and social resources. At the same time cultural studies is also what Barker calls 'non-reductionist'. By this he means that it does not reduce

203 Barker, *Cultural*, p. 8.

the meaning or the significance of a product for audiences to those inscribed at the point of production. For Barker 'political economy, social relationships and culture must be understood in terms of their own specific logics and modes of development'.[204]

Theologians of all kinds are turning to popular culture as a source for reflection and debate. Theological bookstores are starting to feature both popular and academic texts that deal with the 'theology' of a particular band, or with the theological themes in music video, or to discuss the relationship between biblical theology and film. In some churches preachers have started to use film clips and even adverts to illustrate their sermons. The significance of Barker's theme for practical theology is that it draws attention to the role that economic interests play in shaping popular culture. The significance of this is that it encourages a critical engagement with popular culture. At the same time the interests associated with production do not by themselves determine the meaning of a text. A good example of this comes from the use of popular forms of music in contemporary worship. It is possible to critique contemporary worship on the basis that it is spreading a Western form of music and expression around the world, driven by a Christianized form of capitalism, but this is probably much too 'reductive'. This form of analysis needs to be balanced by an understanding of why and how people use these songs in their churches. The way of seeing from cultural studies therefore leads practical theology into a complex engagement with the ways in which representations are produced and how they are used.

Theme 4   Articulation

The concept of articulation expresses the way that relationships are constructed in a social formation. It suggests the way that temporary connections are formed between elements that do not necessarily have to be related. 'Articulation suggests expressing/representating and a putting together.'[205]

Articulation brings to practical theology a way of viewing culture as expression through connections. This way of seeing the cultural

---

204 Barker, *Cultural*, p. 9.
205 Barker, *Cultural*, p. 9.

is particularly helpful in relation to issues of contextualization and inculturation. Contextual theology works by adopting or articulating different elements to make a distinctive expression of faith. A good example of this has been the growth in Christian festivals such as Greenbelt or Soul Survivor. The festival as a cultural form is articulated with theological intentions such as teaching, worship or the exploration of art and faith. Through the form of a festival these theological aims develop a particular cultural form or representation. Articulation, that is, joining the conventions and sensibilities of the festival to the theological area of worship, has an effect on the way that this theological representation is shaped. For practical theology articulation is a particularly helpful way of analysing the cultural. In the first instance it is useful as a way to understand particular formations such as a Christian festival culture and its theological and social effects. Articulation, however, is also significant because it offers an insight into the way in which new expressions of faith and of the Church might take shape. For instance the trend in fresh expression to hold worship services in the local pub is a particular minefield of 'articulation'.

Theme 5 Power

Cultural studies, says Barker, has long been concerned with the question of power. Power is seen as being a part of every social relationship. 'Power is not simply the glue that holds the social together, or the coercive force which subordinates one set of people to another though it certainly is. It is also understood in terms of the processes that generate and enable any form of social action, relationship or order.'[206]

For practical theology this theme of power has a particular significance, for instance in the way that contextual and liberation theologies explore issues of power. Here all forms of representation are seen to take place in relation to the different levels that power is seen to operate. This means that practical theology needs to find ways to read theological representation in relation to the complex interplay of social and political forces. An example of this can be found in the study of congregations where different kinds of power are seen as operating. This may range for instance from the institutional power of elected

---

206 Barker, *Cultural*, p. 9.

individuals on a church council, to the theological power exercised by a leader in a home group, or to the economic power seen in a parish withholding its contribution from its denominational structures. There are also relations of power that operate in churches, for instance in the formal link between the Anglican Church and the state in the UK or the way that particular forms of liturgical expression mirror the structure of a society. There are also the political issues that surround local politics and the role that Christian communities may play in community relations and conflicts.

Theme 6   Popular Culture

For Barker, questions concerning power and subordination are seen as being played out in popular culture. A key issue here relates to the way that popular culture is a site for struggle and 'consent'. So, for example, television news may present the world in terms of 'nations, perceived as naturally occurring objects. This may have the consequence of obscuring both the class divisions of social formations and the constructed character of nationality.'[207] A further example might be the way that advertising can depict women as housewives or as 'sexy bodies alone'.[208]

Practical theology needs to find ways to take popular culture seriously as a place of significance and struggle. This emphasis is crucial in the context of Fresh Expressions of Church. The move towards new kinds of ecclesial life is very often rooted in the adoption of forms of expression found in popular culture. This might be the use of popular music in worship or the use of the internet in facilitating new kinds of Christian community. By adopting these forms of mediation the contemporary Church is locating itself within the contested field of popular culture. There is therefore a real need to frame these developments theologically through a nuanced understanding of culture and how it operates to shape identity and difference. A critical appreciation of popular culture is particularly significant if ministers and believers are to be encouraged to develop a prophetic relationship to popular culture.

---

207 Barker, *Cultural*, p. 10.
208 Barker, *Cultural*, p. 10.

Theme 7   Texts and Readers

Texts relate not simply to the written word but to 'all signifying practices'.[209] Barker says that texts in this sense include: images, sounds, clothes as well as activities such as dance or sport. Readers may deal with texts in different ways, for instance the interpretation of texts by textual critics may differ from those of participants or audiences. Yet meaning cannot be simply 'read off the audience'. Meaning is 'produced in an interplay between text and reader'. And so the moment of consumption is also a point of meaningful production.[210]

The dynamic interaction between audiences and texts in the construction of meaning is a particularly fruitful area for theological reflection. Practical theology can find in cultural studies a way to view the theological through this dynamic. An example of this kind of analysis is found in hymnology. The meaning of a hymn such as William Blake's 'Jerusalem' cannot be read from its lyric alone. The meaning of 'Jerusalem' is found in the complex interplay between its use and its text. 'Jerusalem' may mean different things as it is used in different contexts. So its meaning may shift as it is used for instance at a funeral, or sung at a rugby match or in the chapel of a public school. None of these meanings may correspond precisely with the way that 'Jerusalem' might be interpreted by a literary critic who is primarily concerned with the interpretation of the poem as part of Blake's wider literary and artistic work.

Theme 8   Subjectivity and Identity

Cultural studies has been particularly concerned with questions of identity. This has meant, for example, the exploration of the subject and how identities are shaped by representations of what it means to be male, female, black, young or old. Identities relate to discursive constructions, 'they are the product of discourses or regulated ways of speaking, notably languages'.[211]

The culture of Christian communities needs to be a major emphasis

---

209 Barker, *Culture*, p. 10.
210 Barker, *Culture*, p. 10.
211 Barker, *Culture*, p. 11.

in practical theology. The shift towards the cultural means that theological expressions of Christian tradition must be seen as forces that shape individual and communal forms of Christian identity within the church context. The participation of individuals in the cultural expression or language of faith is therefore read through this lens as identity formation. So what it means to be a Catholic will be in part shaped in relation to the way that Catholic doctrine, liturgical convention and tradition act to form the believer.

Circuit(s) of Culture

Barker's key themes in cultural studies are often presented as a circuit of interrelated stages of interpretation. An example of this way of structuring the study of culture as a series of stages or a circuit is Chris Rojek's 'sphere of culture'.[212] Understanding cultural studies as a circuit has gained widespread acceptance, but the circuit is often represented in slightly different ways.[213] Richard Johnson, Deborah Chambers, Pravati Raghuram and Estella Tincknell present a version of the circuit as: text, reading, everyday life, and production. This version of the circuit, they argue, is particularly relevant to a consideration of face-to-face exchanges or forms such as television programmes or useful and meaningful objects such as the personal hi-fi. In this model 'everyday life' marks both a starting point and a returning point for cultural analysis. Cultural producers make representations as texts, these are in turn read, and these readings have consequences in everyday life.[214] They make a link between this idea of the circuit of culture and the hermeneutics of Paul Ricoeur.

For Ricoeur hermeneutics is distinct from semiotics or structural analysis because it is concerned with 'reconstructing the entire arc of operations by which practical experience provides itself with works, authors and readers'.[215] Johnson and his co-authors argue that Ricoeur's arc is similar to the circuit of culture. The arc is structured around three moments of mimesis. The first moment, 'prefiguration', is based on the

---

212 Rojek, *Cultural*, p. 12.
213 See Johnson, *Practice*, p. 37.
214 Johnson, *Practice*, p. 38.
215 Ricoeur, quoted in Johnson, *Practice*, p. 38.

assumption that the narratives of life precede representation. 'Storytelling arises from human acting and suffering.'[216] The second moment, or 'configuration', refers to cultural production and encoding. The third moment of mimesis Ricoeur labels as 'refiguration'. Here he focuses on the productive work of readers. The practice of reading unifies the three moments. 'Three aspects are involved here: there are traditions of storytelling that are shared between writers and readers; there is the act of reading itself, which revises what the author gives the reader; there is the reader's life, which is also changed.'[217] The link to Ricoeur is significant because it demonstrates how the 'way of seeing' associated with cultural studies, illustrated through circuits of culture, forms part of a much wider intellectual movement towards the cultural.

In *Doing Cultural Studies: The Story of the Sony Walkman*, Paul du Gay, Stuart Hall, Linda Janes, Hugh Mackay and Keith Negus present the cultural circuit as comprising five 'cultural processes'.[218] Their model of interpretation is based on the articulation of a number of distinct processes, 'whose interaction can and does lead to variable and contingent outcomes'.[219] Articulation expresses the way that these processes are linked in a way that is not necessary or determined or absolute or essential 'for all time'.[220] The five processes that form the basis for their reading of the Sony Walkman are: representation, identity, production, consumption and regulation. To study an artefact such as the Walkman, they argue, cultural analysis should pass through and explore 'how it is represented, what social identities are associated with it, how it is produced and consumed and what mechanisms regulate its distribution and use'.[221] The circuit expresses the idea that it is only through a consideration of the articulation of these processes that an explanation can be found. As a circuit it is not necessary to start at any particular point; however, it is important to pass through each of the stages. In addition to this they suggest that in each of the moments in the circuit the other moments are also taken up and form part of the

---

216 Johnson, *Practice*, p. 38.
217 Johnson, *Practice*, p. 38.
218 Du Gay, P., Hall, S., Janes, L., Mackay, H. and Negus, K. (1997), *Doing Cultural Studies: The Story of the Sony Walkman*, London: Sage, p. 3.
219 Du Gay, *Doing*, p. 3.
220 Du Gay, *Doing*, p. 3.
221 Du Gay, *Doing*, p. 3.

understanding. One of the reasons for this is that the separation of the processes is an interpretative construction in 'real life' and so they are seen as forming part of a whole.[222]

Practical Theology and the Circuit of Culture

Cultural studies has evolved as a way of seeing that has been adopted across a range of academic disciplines. The circuit of culture is a way of structuring this way of seeing that can be used in practical theology. The following chapters make use of a simplified form of the circuit as a way of doing practical theology. This simplified form reads culture by moving through three moments of interpretation: production, representation (or text) and audience (or consumption). In the next chapter these three moments are explained through the way that popular music studies has been shaped around production, text and audience. This interpretative framework is then used as a way of reading a popular worship song.

---

222 Du Gay, *Doing*, p. 4.

4

Production, Text and Audience: 'Shine, Jesus, shine'

Given the flood of interest in theology and film, it is perhaps surprising that very little has been written on theology and popular music studies.[223] Pop music can appear to elude theological engagement: where film has a capacity for narrative, plot and characterization, we have to accept that the three-minute pop song is inevitably less complex and textured and as such it 'affords' less within theological debate. At the same time, popular music is much more omnipresent than film. Pop songs are seamlessly interwoven with our experience of life. It is no exaggeration to say that pop songs function as a 'sound track to our lives', and it is music, rather than film, that has shaped individual identities and youth cultures.

The significance of pop music in everyday life means that there is a compelling reason why it should be a particular focus for practical theology. Understanding how identity and difference is marked through musical style and taste is not just a prerequisite for the youth minister but it is increasingly important for ministry with people of all ages. As churches start to introduce popular styles of music into worship, this is an area that requires sustained and quite urgent theological attention. This chapter uses popular music studies to explore in more depth the 'way of seeing' that has its origins in cultural studies. From the study of popular music a simplified form of the cultural circuit is then used as the basis for an analysis of Graham Kendrick's popular worship song 'Shine, Jesus, shine'. This examination of 'Shine, Jesus, shine' shows how cultural perspectives can allow practical theology to form

---

223 For an exception to this, see Gilmour, M. J. (ed.) (2005), *Call Me the Seeker: Listening to Religion in Popular Music*, London: Continuum.

a complex reading of the theological significance of a popular worship song. This interpretation draws on a version of the cultural circuit that comes from both media studies and cultural studies. In cultural studies, as we saw in the last chapter, a pattern of analysis has developed based around culture as representation, production, and consumption.[224] In media studies, analysis is often divided between a consideration of media texts, how those texts are produced through the action of media institutions, and how texts are received by audiences. This leads to a threefold pattern similar to that in cultural studies of: institution, text and audience. In media studies this form of the cultural circuit is used to shape the discussion of most kinds of media.[225] These categories in cultural and media studies are largely interchangeable.

Production	Representation	Consumption
Institution	Text	Audience

Music as Production Text and Audience

The way of seeing developed within cultural studies concerning the nature and interpretation of culture has been widely taken up in the study of contemporary popular music. In particular the discussion of the relationship between culture industry, audience consumption and identities, and the meaning of the text, have been carried from cultural studies into the consideration of popular music. Brian Longhurst argues that the study of popular music should be based around this pattern. Cultural objects, he argues, should be viewed as texts, but these texts result from the activity of production processes. The production of texts takes place through the operation of a variety of institutions. Production may be relatively simple, or in the case of a record extremely complex.[226]

224 Hall's circuit of culture also includes 'regulation', that is, the means whereby the marketing and consumption of cultural products are regulated by governments and the like. For the sake of clarity and brevity I have chosen not to include this phase of analysis here.

225 For an account of research methods in cultural studies see Johnson, *Practice*; Barker, *Cultural*; and du Gay, *Doing*.

226 Longhurst, B. (1995), *Popular Music and Society*, Cambridge: Polity Press, p. 22.

Thus, a record will be the outcome of a complex set of procedures involving different people and social processes, including musicians, recording engineers, record producers, playing instruments, interaction in a recording studio, mixing tapes, the manufacture of records in a factory and so on.[227]

As well as being produced, records are also consumed. It is therefore important, says Longhurst, to examine the means and methods by which audiences consume or 'read' popular music.[228] He explores the sequence of production, text and audience, under five areas of enquiry for the sociological examination of popular music.[229] The first area involves questions concerning the methods of production and the role of the producer. Here Longhurst argues that cultural studies should explore the production of popular music and the way that producers are located within social and economic systems. Closely related to this are the ways that producers may, or may not, exercise control over artists or music. The second area involves questions relating to how production takes place, and examines who produces music and the nature of that production. The processes of production are essential to understanding the nature of popular music, and associated with this is the way that power and control may be exercised through production processes. Third, there are a number of issues related to understanding music as text. These include the variety of approaches to the methods by which texts are to be analysed and interpreted. Fourth, there are issues related to what is meant by the term audience. The social make-up of the audience for a particular song or group may therefore be examined, and the ways that audiences make use of the music may be discussed. In particular, how 'texts produce certain identifications for us when we watch, read or listen to them'.[230] Fifth, Longhurst argues that the manner in which texts are consumed should be examined. The meaning of music can be affected if it is primarily listened to on a Walkman or at a disco or on the radio, if the person listens on their

---

227 Longhurst, *Popular*, p. 22.
228 See O'Sullivan, T., Hartley, J., Saunders, D., Montgomery, M. and Fiske, J. (1994), *Key Concepts in Communication and Cultural Studies*, London: Routledge, p. 20.
229 Longhurst, *Popular*, p. 22.
230 Longhurst, *Popular*, p. 23.

own, in their bedroom, or socially, at concerts, or in a pub. Thus, 'The detail of social context', he says, 'can have a great effect on the meaning and form of appropriation of a text.'[231]

Longhurst's five questions involve a complex structuring of the study of popular music around production, text and consumption, and the relationships that develop around these three areas. At the same time he is also concerned that cultural analysis should maintain a separation between these three areas. Separation is essential so that a detailed examination of each area might take place but also in order that the relationships between areas might be better understood.[232] Roy Shuker approaches popular music in a similar way to Longhurst. He argues that a variety of interpretations and meanings are located in the recordings and performances associated with popular music. These meanings, he says, are in one sense the creation of those who have made the music. At the same time meaning results from the way that consumers interact with these texts. A third element is that the texts and performances are themselves 'cultural commodities'. These cultural commodities are the products of a multi-national industry that is dedicated to maximising profit.[233] The nature of popular music therefore means that interpretation involves an examination of all of these areas and a consideration of their relationship.

> Meanings, or rather, particular sets of cultural understandings, are the result of a complex set of interactions between these different parties. Accordingly the question of meaning in rock can only be satisfactorily answered by considering the nature of production context, including State cultural policy, the texts and their creators, and the audience. Most importantly, it is necessary to consider the inter-relationship of these factors.[234]

Robert Walser's *Running With the Devil* deals with heavy metal music by prioritizing the production associated with musicians, and

---

231 Longhurst, *Popular*, p. 23.
232 Longhurst, *Popular*, p. 249. A similar position is advocated by Roy Shuker: see Shuker, R. (1994), *Understanding Popular Music*, London: Routledge.
233 Shuker, *Understanding*, viii.
234 Shuker, *Understanding*, viii.

along with music and performance, that is read as text: 'As a musician, I cannot help but think that individual texts, and the social experiences they represent, are important.'[235] He develops his approach by adopting Christopher Small's notion of 'musicking'. According to Small, music is not a 'thing' but an activity in which we engage.[236] By speaking of music as an activity Small focuses less upon content than upon the 'act' and 'event' which he sums up in his creation of the term 'musicking'. If music is an activity then textual analysis gives way to questions concerning the meanings that are created when a performance takes place in a particular time and in a particular place.[237] Small argues that the focus for analysing meaning in music should therefore be the relationships that are established when a performance takes place.[238] Thus for Small there are three elements to 'musicking' which are seen in the relationships which surround the sound event. First, the exploration of identity; second, the participation in what he calls an 'ideal society'; and third, the modelling of relationships within that ideal society.[239] A musical performance is thus 'a ritual in which is acted out the mythology of a social group'.[240] Walser argues that the term 'musicking' allows for an understanding of music that is wide-ranging and does justice both to musicians and audience. '"Musicking" embraces composition, performance, listening, dancing – all of the social practices of which musical scores are merely one dimensional traces.'[241]

The work of Walser, Longhurst and others shows that there is a pattern of interpretation within the study of popular music based on the framework of production, text and audience. This means that questions related to the meaning and significance of a musical text must take account of the complex interaction between productive processes, the content of the text itself and the ways in which this text is consumed. This pattern of interpretation offers a framework for

---

235 Walser, R. (1993), *Running with the Devil: Power, Gender and Madness in Heavy Metal Music*, New England: Wesleyan University Press, p. xii.
236 Small, C. (1987), *Music of the Common Tongue*, London: Calder Riverrun, p. 50.
237 Small, *Music*, p. 51.
238 Small, *Music*, p. 62.
239 Small, *Music*, p. 74.
240 Small, *Music*, p. 75.
241 Walser, *Running*, p. xiii.

approaching all forms of popular music including contemporary forms of worship. I want to illustrate how practical theology can make use of an interpretative framework based around these three areas by using them to develop a complex reading of a song that is frequently used in contemporary worship: 'Shine, Jesus, shine'.

Shine Jesus Shine: Production and Text

Written in 1987, Graham Kendrick's, 'Shine, Jesus, shine' has been one of the most popular and widely used songs from the charismatic renewal.[242] Over the last twenty years, 'Shine, Jesus, shine' has consistently appeared among the top ten most popular worship songs in the UK and in the US Christian worship charts.[243] 'Shine, Jesus, shine' is a rare example of a song from the present-day charismatic worship scene that has crossed over not only into the mainstream Church but also into non-church contexts. Over the years it has been sung at a wide range of events, including the memorial service for those killed in Dunblane and the memorial for those massacred in Tasmania; it has also been sung at Billy Graham crusades and at one of the largest ever open air masses with the Pope in Manila.[244]

> Lord, the light of your love is shining
> In the midst of the darkness, shining
> Jesus, Light of the world, shine upon us
> Set us free by the truth you now bring us
> Shine on me, shine on me
>
> Shine, Jesus, shine
> Fill this land with the Father's glory
> Blaze, Spirit, blaze
> Set our hearts on fire

---

242 Kendrick, G. (2001), *Behind the Songs*, Stowmarket: Kevin Mayhew, p. 152.

243 Christian Copyright Licensing International (CCLI) produce a 'pop chart' based on the number of times songs are used in churches, schools and other licensed venues; see http://www.ccli.co.uk/ accessed 20 June 2007.

244 http://www.grahamkendrick.co.uk/insight/story/story_shine.htm accessed 20 June 2007.

Flow, river, flow
Flood the nations with grace and mercy
Send forth your word Lord,
and let there be light

Lord, I come to your awesome presence
From the shadows into your radiance
By the blood I may enter your brightness
Search me, try me, consume all my darkness
Shine on me, shine on me

As we gaze on your kingly brightness
So our faces display your likeness
Ever changing from glory to glory
Mirrored here may our lives tell your story
Shine on me, shine on me[245]

'Shine, Jesus, shine' is 'produced', and so like other popular songs it is inscribed with meaning by its production. The lyric draws directly upon Pauline imagery from 2 Corinthians, but 'Shine, Jesus, shine' locates the transforming light of Christ in an immediate and present moment. The truth is brought 'now'. As 'we' gaze on Christ 'we' are changed from glory to glory. The 'we' in 'Shine, Jesus, shine' positions the singer in an embodied, enacted and realized theology. It is as the worshipper sings that hearts are set on fire, the Spirit blazes and the glory is 'mirrored' here. Place and spatial imagery are central to the song. It is in the midst of darkness that the light shines, and through the blood 'I may enter your brightness'. It is 'this land' that is filled with the Father's glory, and nations who are to be flooded with 'grace and mercy' as the word is 'sent forth'.

The song forms part of what Graham Kendrick calls a 'liturgy for the streets'.[246] He explains in his book *Behind the Songs* that the origins of 'Shine, Jesus, shine' lie in the practice of public praise developed by the Ichthus Fellowship, a group of charismatic churches based

---

245 Graham Kendrick, Copyright © 1987 Make Way Music. Used by permission.
246 Kendrick, *Behind*, p. 155.

in London.[247] During the early 1980s Ichthus began to explore the idea of taking the worship of their church onto the streets to create a new kind of public worship. The idea was to eventually give birth to the worldwide movement known as 'The March for Jesus'. Kendrick records that he first wrote the verses at a time when the Church was teaching on the presence and holiness of God and only later added the chorus. 'Shine, Jesus, shine' formed a part of a larger group of songs, which were all to be used as part of the public praise ministry of the Church. For Kendrick the practice of public praise comes from a particular charismatic theology:

> For me the March for Jesus concept emerged out of my exploration of worship and my experience as a Worship leader ... I found that many Christian groups were discovering a great rise of faith or sense of spiritual breakthrough as a result of praise that proclaimed truth. I became interested in the dynamics of praise and its relation to prayer and spiritual warfare.[248]

Kendrick did not see the marches as a kind of ecclesiastical publicity stunt or Christian protest movement, rather they were a spiritual practice of obedience.[249] Christian people, says Kendrick, are called to worship and offer God their praises. Praise is transformative when it is offered on the streets, where God is rarely worshipped. Christians take a relationship with God onto the streets, and in worship they celebrate his presence. 'He is actually there, where considerably more than two or three are gathered in His name, and we lavish upon Him the love of our hearts before people and angels.'[250] 'Marching for Jesus is not a method of spiritual warfare but as Christians are obedient in worship and celebrate the presence of God in relationship', says Kendrick, and 'as we put our feet down in His name, we may find that whether consciously or not we have trodden upon "serpents and scorpions".'[251]

---

247 For the origins of the Ichthus Fellowship, see Walker, A. (1998), *Restoring the Kingdom: The Radical Christianity of the House Church Movement*, Guildford: Eagle.

248 Kendrick, G., Coates, G., Forster, R. and Green, L. (1992), *March for Jesus*, Eastbourne: Kingsway, p. 24.

249 Kendrick, G. (1992), *Shine Jesus Shine*, Milton Keynes: Word Books, p. 24.

250 Kendrick, *Shine*, p. 27.

251 Kendrick, *Shine*, p. 30.

'Shine, Jesus, shine' is a particular representation, which arises from Kendrick's participation in the enacted theology of the Ichthus Fellowship and the wider charismatic subculture. Within the discourses of the community this theology is generated and embodied through an experimental and dynamic process. In its original setting it formed a part of a liturgy of the streets where charismatic Christians understood themselves to be celebrating the transforming presence of God in their midst. This transformation was not simply understood as being personal or confined to the Christian community. The act of worship released the power of God to blaze in the nation and heal the land. By marching in public they took this transforming presence outside the walls of their churches and mediated it in the wider society. Their performance of worship was a spiritual force, which connected them to the angels and caused demons to flee.

'Shine, Jesus, Shine' as Production, Mediation and Consumption

'Shine, Jesus, shine' formed part of a much larger group of songs and materials, which Kendrick produced to resource the developing movement of praise marches. He promoted these materials through his company Make Way, which was launched in 1986. Kendrick describes his motivation for developing the Make Way materials. 'I see my job as providing churches with resources so that, on any day of the year they deem suitable, they have some musical tools to take out onto the streets. For me that was a specific strategy and the reason I began to multiply Make Way resources.'[252] 'Shine, Jesus, shine' and the other resources were therefore commodified and marketed to stimulate a specific vision for public worship. Through the March for Jesus organization millions of Christians around the world were to embrace public worship in what became a popular movement.[253] Yet 'Shine, Jesus, shine' has had a life way beyond public praise.

The Christian worship scene around the world is characterized by an enormous range of media-based products: worship recordings on CDs, internet-based downloads and websites selling resources, magazines,

---

252 Kendrick, *March*, p. 25.
253 See Kendrick, *March*, for an account of the rapid growth in the March for Jesus.

radio stations and Christian TV stations. All of the mediations deliver a percentage of their takings as a royalty, and these are collected by the CCLI. The fact that 'Shine, Jesus, shine' has remained in the CCLI chart for 20 years is an indication of its widespread use throughout the Christian community. The processes of production and reproduction utilized by the charismatic worship industry mean that a song like 'Shine, Jesus, shine' can be taken up by a wide variety of churches. At a grassroots level this means that the song has found a place in the regular worship of the majority of churches who subscribe to a CCLI licence. It is consumed as local churches sing the song, and as worship leaders play it. This inevitably means that its commodification has enabled the song to travel beyond the specific theological and charismatic setting from which it emerged. A consideration of the theological and ecclesial production of the song does not therefore circumscribe its meaning, because every time 'Shine, Jesus, shine' is used in an act of worship it is relocated in the new context. This means that Kendrick's particular take on the theology of charismatic worship does not necessarily limit the potential for the song through articulation to take on new meanings.

Every act of worship is similar to Small's 'musicking'. It is a performance where texts, artists and congregations interact to make a meaningful event. When it is used as part of an act of worship 'Shine, Jesus, shine' is repositioned in a new performance alongside other texts. This may include liturgies, other songs, prayers, sermons, rituals, architecture, and so on. The meaning of the song can shift in this new context as it is repositioned in a variety of symbolic theological and ecclesial ecosystems. The use of 'Shine, Jesus, shine' at Dunblane and in Tasmania is interesting from this perspective. In these memorial services the song is relocated in the context of national tragedy and mourning. The meaning of the song, as it is read from production alone, may not encapsulate its meaning for these congregations. It is therefore not possible to interpret the meaning of the text by simply analysing the lyrics of the song and the way that it was produced from within a particular theological context. Production and text must be supplemented by performance and the ways in which individuals and communities identify with the song as it is performed.

Finally, it is important to note that the model of production, text and audience shifts in relation to the performance of 'Shine, Jesus, shine' as part of a worship event. In performance the song is linked in another representation or texts, which can also be read and interpreted in a variety of ways. Acts of worship are themselves representation and texts that are in turn 'produced' by clergy, worship leaders, theological traditions, and so on. At the same time, performance also relates to the way that people make meaning in relation to worship. This wider performance of worship and its significance for the methods of enquiry appropriate for practical theology is explored in more detail in the next part through a discussion of the service of Holy Communion or the Eucharist as production, representation and audience.

Part 2

Participation and Mediation

5

Participation

The convergence on culture marks a significant move in practical theology. Turning to culture means that doctrine is increasingly read in and
through the social and the embodied and so 'theology' itself is seen in
a new light. This means that the cultural effectively transforms theological method. From the point of view of the practitioner this move towards culture is reassuring. It encourages a form of practical theology
that respects the place of doctrine and theology as it is embodied in
communities and lived in as tradition. This link between doctrine and
practice means that practical theology is able to develop critical theory
that is much closer to the expression of the Church. As a result this
approach to theology is not only more accessible to the practitioner, it
is also more hospitable. Yet for all that can be gained from this there
are inherent problems in the cultural turn.

The turn introduces a direction of travel that tends to encourage the
view that 'theology' should be read as part of the cultural expression of
the Christian community. The temptation then is to present practical
theology as an academic and critical reflection on this cultural expression of the Church. There is a problem with this because although it is
true to say that 'theology' is cultural it is also and at the same time more
than culture. Faith is lived in as an embodied and communal participation in the theological. So theology functions as culture or as a way of
life and yet it cannot be reduced to culture. Faith is lived in but it is also
indwelt by God. It is precisely this lived-in and indwelt nature of the
theological that is conveyed by the terms participation and mediation.

Participation refers both to a communion in the divine life and to
a sharing in the cultural expression of the Church. Mediation relates
to the way that expression becomes a place of divine indwelling and
presence through the operation of various forms and processes of

cultural communication. It is this element of divine indwelling as it is mediated in cultural and theological expression that transforms practical theology from a distanced or uncommitted academic practice into a spiritual discipline.

Trinity and Participation

The suggestion that practical theology should be seen as a spiritual discipline finds its force in a particular understanding of 'theology' as a participation in the Trinitarian life of God. In contemporary theological thought a link between participation and relationality in the Church and a communion in the divine being has become quite commonplace, but it is particularly associated with the work of John Zizioulas.[254] Zizioulas develops his discussion of the Church and of God through the category of being or ontology. He argues that the being of God is to be understood in and through ideas of relationship and community. Thus for Zizioulas ecclesial identity, or ecclesial being, indicates an ultimate reality which rests on God mediated in communion.[255] So he argues that, 'The mystery of the Church, even in its institutional dimension, is deeply bound to the very being of man, to the being of the world and to the very being of God.'[256] As a member of the Church the believer is in the 'image of God', says Zizioulas.[257] It was this ecclesial experience of communion which generated and directed the thinking of the early church fathers. Ecclesial identity and communion was of particular significance, he says, for Athanasius and Irenaeus, in their consideration of the being of God. 'This experience revealed something very important: the being of God could be known only through personal relationships and personal love. Being means life and life means communion.'[258] So, for Zizioulas, the ontology of the fathers, that is, their understanding of the being of God, emerges out of the eucharistic life

---

254 Zizioulas, J. (1985), *Being As Communion: Studies in Personhood and the Church*, Crestwood, NY: Saint Valdimir's Seminary Press.

255 Olson, R. E. and Hall, C. A (2002), *The Trinity*, Grand Rapids: Eerdmans, p. 113.

256 Zizioulas, *Being*, 15.

257 Zizioulas, *Being*, 15.

258 Zizioulas, *Being*, 16.

of the Church. Communion and being are therefore dynamically and relationally connected. Thus he asserts that 'God has no ontological content, no true being, apart from communion.'[259]

Communion therefore makes things be. Without communion nothing exists, including God. In communion, and by this he means in the Eucharist, the Church contemplates the life of the Holy Trinity as communion. In such contemplation lay the realization of humanity's true being as an 'image of God's own being'.[260] Thus the Eucharist is not the practice of a Church which already exists, rather it is the Eucharist that 'constitutes the Church's being'.[261] Participation in communion is participation in the very life of God. 'The life of the Eucharist is the life of God Himself ... It is the life of *communion* with God, such as exists within the Trinity and is actualised within the members of the Eucharistic community.'[262] Thus, says Zizioulas, 'Knowledge and communion are identical.'[263] This, according to Alan Torrance, is the strength of Zizioulas's position. 'Divine communication in the context of faith is an event of communion and demands to be conceived, therefore, in terms of participation within communion (and hence the "mutuality") of the triune life.'[264]

Zizioulas is not alone among contemporary theologians in making the link between ecclesial identity, the being of the Church, and the being of God. While he expresses reservations about Zizioulas's understanding of communion in the Church, Miroslav Volf does approve of what he calls, 'a social understanding of salvation'. He identifies this version of 'social salvation' as being held in common within the Catholic and the Orthodox traditions of the Church as exemplified by Zizioulas and Rahner respectively.[265] David Cunningham is also in general agreement with these judgements; he observes that, despite differences over the meaning and the use of terminology, the link

---

259 Zizioulas, *Being*, 17.
260 Zizioulas, *Being*, 21.
261 Zizioulas, *Being*, 21.
262 Zizioulas, *Being*, 81.
263 Zizioulas, *Being*, 81.
264 Torrance, A. (1996), *Persons in Communion: Trinitarian Description and Human Participation*, Edinburgh: T & T Clark, p. 288.
265 Volf, M. (1998), *After Our Likeness: The Church as the Image of the Trinity*, Grand Rapids: Eerdmans, p. 172.

between relationality and the being of God as they are advocated by Zizioulas is widely shared in contemporary Trinitarian theology.[266]

A relational understanding of the Trinity as being in communion is extended to the life of the Christian community through the idea of participation. Expression and communication within the Church becomes a mediation of divine life. For Paul Fiddes this communicative dynamic means that the notion of 'representation' lies at the heart of Zizioulas's work.[267] Fiddes points out that communion and communication are integral to a relational and participative Trinitarian theology. Torrance also makes this kind of link between communion and communication. He argues that in the debate on analogy, Zizioulas's theology of participation, his 'analysis of capacity and incapacity, and his relating of communion and communication, personhood and truthfulness', are profoundly significant.[268]

This Trinitarian theology of participation and mediation means that the cultural expression of the Church is seen as a place of divine encounter. The link between the being of God and the expression of the Christian community transforms the understanding of practical theology. The communication of the Church can be read as culture but it is also and at the same time a place of divine indwelling. Theological expression is therefore linked to the being of God, and to share in this expression is to be in communion. The link between expression and communion is particularly significant for practical theology because it suggests that within this kind of Trinitarian thinking the expression of 'theology' becomes a place of mediation and encounter. In other words it cannot be dealt with solely within the reductive categories of rational abstraction or cultural analysis without an adequate account being offered of 'theology' as the mediation of divine being. This means that practical theology must locate itself as a spiritual discipline of rational and critical interaction with the expression of the Church.

There is one further implication of participative understanding of theology. If theological expression is a mediation of divine presence then practical theology shares in this communion. In other words

---

266 See Cunningham, D. S. (1998), *These Three are One: The Practice of Trinitarian Theology*, Oxford: Blackwell, pp. 26–30.
267 Fiddes, *Participating*, p. 52.
268 Torrance, *Persons*, p. 305.

practical theology should see itself as a part of the ongoing representation and expression of the Christian community. So practical theology is also participation and mediation, which is to say, an indwelling and a being indwelt. In exploring further this approach to practical theology as a spiritual practice of participation and mediation I want to draw upon what has become a classic starting point in the discussion of the nature of theology: Anselm's treatment of theology as 'faith seeking understanding'.

Faith Seeking Understanding

Karl Barth argued that Anselm's 'faith seeking understanding' indicates that the being of God precedes our knowing of God. Thus for Barth our knowing rests on the being of God who is Trinity and the being of God structures theological reason. Barth therefore reads Anselm's theological quest as the search of faith. Faith seeking understanding is an intellectual knowledge, which consists of a 'positive meditation'.[269] This observation is particularly significant for practical theology. It focuses attention on theological reflection as a meditation that is the pursuit of God whose being precedes our pursuing. Anselm's opening lines in *Proslogion* demonstrate his understanding of the way that rationality and reflection function as meditation:

> Come now, insignificant man, leave behind for a time your preoccupations; seclude yourself for a while from your disquieting thoughts. Turn aside now from heavy cares and disregard your wearisome tasks. Attend for a while to God and rest for a time in him. Enter the inner chamber of your mind and shut out all else except God and whatever is of aid to you in seeking him; after closing the door think upon your God. Speak now my heart where and how to seek you, where and how to find you. If you are not here, Lord, where shall I seek you in your absence? But if you are everywhere, why do I not behold you in your presence? Surely you dwell in light inaccessible.[270]

---

269 Barth, K. (1960), *Anselm: Fides Quaerens Intellectum*, trans. Robertson, I. W., London: SCM Press, p. 39.

270 Anselm (1974), 'Proslogion', in Hopkins, J. and Richardson, H. W. (trans.), *Anselm of Canterbury*, vol. 1, London: SCM Press, p. 91.

For Anselm the theological search for understanding is preceded by faith. Faith is represented in these lines by the practice of prayer. Rationality in the *Proslogion* is therefore an intentional spiritual discipline. It involves setting aside the immediate cares and concerns of life and finding a place for contemplation and meditation. Here theological reflection is presented as a reflexive religious culture. The writer is exhorting the reader to rest in God. Rest in this sense does not mean that the problems of practice are set to one side. Anselm seeks a place of contemplation to wrestle with his concerns, and this wrestling is simultaneously the pursuit of God. This is not a form of pietistic escapism and should not be interpreted as such. I want to suggest that the place of 'rest' should be interpreted as a spiritual discipline within which the tensions and contradictions of practice are situated as a participation in the divine life. Anselm's *Proslogion* indicates that we can see practical theology as a spiritual practice. Here theological reasoning is cultural in that it is a spiritual practice that is 'lived-in', but it is simultaneously a place of divine encounter. Reflection is concerned with rationality, but it is also a place of prayer that is indwelt by God. It is *faith* that is seeking understanding.

Faith seeking understanding locates practical theology as a form of reason that involves a spiritual discipline and practice. For the ministerial practitioner Anselm represents a familiar purchase on the theological task because his theological questions are located in an embodied practice of divine presence. Prayer and puzzlement often coexist for the minister. The problems faced in ministry shape our prayer as much as our prayer shapes our ministry. We may be wrestling with the problem of expressing faith in a media-orientated pluralistic culture rather than, like Anselm, working on the ontological argument for the existence of God, but we approach these issues in much the same way, as people of faith. Faith and being faithful mean that our questions often go hand in hand with our prayer. With Anselm we seek to rest with our questions in the presence of God. When practical theology is situated as an embodied spiritual practice and a discipline of divine encounter it relocates itself in the recognizable and everyday practice of the minister. It grows from this inhabited space where the social and the doctrinal coexist and co-inhere. This is an embodied space, which is simultaneously lived in and indwelt. It is a practical theology that is both participation and mediation.

Reflection: Lived in and Indwelt

Ministers do not generally engage in practical theology simply for the sake of gaining understanding or even just for purely pragmatic solutions to ministerial problems. Theology is concerned with both of these things but above all it is about God. In fact the theological task is 'theology' because it is the pursuit of God. Faith seeks understanding and this is an inhabited place of encounter and transformation. Practical theology as participation and mediation recognizes that faith seeks understanding in pursuit of faith, that is, it seeks a transforming encounter with God. It starts with an embodied, lived-in and indwelt moment, it passes through a lived-in and indwelt rationality, and it returns to a transformed practice and expression of faith. Theological reflection is therefore a practice of reason and it is also and at the same time a mediation of the divine life. Practical theology is therefore the practice of reason as a spiritual discipline that mediates the divine presence. Reflection is thus located in a participation in the divine presence. This approach to practical theology as a spiritual discipline of participation is theological 'reflection' because it mediates the divine presence. Reflection is reflection because it has its origins in God who is present. So it is possible to speak about reflection as being related to the divine light or divine glory. A starting point for this theological discussion of reflection is found in a passage from St Paul's Second Letter to the Corinthians.

> Now the Lord is the Spirit, and where the Spirit of the Lord is, there is freedom. And all of us, with unveiled faces, seeing the glory of the Lord as though reflected in a mirror, are being transformed into the same image from one degree of glory to another; for this comes from the Lord, the Spirit.[271]

Paul is obviously not talking about any contemporary form of practical theology, but it is the idea of 'reflection' that is suggestive. Reflection, as Paul speaks of it, reframes the task of practical theology by situating Anselm's exhortation to commence the theological task, by drawing aside and resting a while in God, within a dynamic

---

271 2 Cor. 3.17-18.

Trinitarian flow of reflected glory. In St Paul's thinking reflection is the freedom of the Lord who is the Spirit. Glory or *doxa* denotes the presence of God. As Jervell says, the divine *doxa* is the way God exists and acts. The *doxa* of Christ therefore refers to the presence of God in Christ.[272] Thus the glory of the Lord speaks of the presence of God in Christ and through the work of the Spirit in the believer. This is the freedom brought by the Spirit, for the believer may see with an unveiled face and therefore reflect this glory. The Spirit is the presence of God and the transforming power of God.[273] Reflection therefore comes from God and it returns to God. It is a mystical participation, a divine indwelling. So through exercise of theological reflection practical theology may be focused on the social and cultural forms of faith but it is simultaneously seeking God in and through these things. This does not mean that God is reduced to the cultural or the social. Reflection as the freedom of the Spirit locates both of these in divine encounter. It is those with unveiled faces who are free. So there is an unveiling in practical theology when the cultural and the theological become a place of encounter. Reflection in practical theology clearly involves academic practices and the conventions of rational thought and debate. As such it is lived in as a cultural practice but it is also and at the same time the freedom of the Spirit that takes these up and transforms them as a place of indwelling. So practical theology is theology (that is, faith seeking after God that is also a participation in God) because it is reflection in the freedom of the Spirit. The freedom of the Spirit is the expression of the divine mission, the transforming of humanity, through a participation in reflected glory, into the image of God.

Mission of God

Reflection is a participation or sharing in the Trinitarian life. It is therefore also a participation or sharing in the mission of God. The minister who seeks to reflect theologically does so from an embodied commitment. Commitment for the minister is not simply a task, or

---

272 J. Jervell quoted in Barrett, C. K. (1973), *A Commentary on The Second Letter to the Corinthians*, London: A & C Black, p. 132.

273 Fee, G. (1994), *God's Empowering Presence: The Holy Spirit in the Letters of Paul*, Peabody: Hendrickson, p. 309.

a professional role. Neither is it simply a sense of self or of communal identity, it is a vocation, a calling. So the theological task forms a part of an active and vocational participation in the mission of God. Mission finds its origins and its energy in God.

Mission, says David Bosch, is 'God's self revelation as the one who loves the world, God's involvement in and with the world, the nature and activity of God, which embraces both the church and the good news that God is a God-for-people'.[274] The mission and ministry of the Church is therefore located in God, who is Trinity. This means that the mission of the Church is an expression of the divine sending forth of the self, the sending of the Son and the Holy Spirit to the world.[275] In reflection we do not simply observe but we are transformed into this Trinitarian life. Reflection therefore arises from and in turn energizes mission, and to reflect theologically is to be taken into this missional life of God. So reflection comes from the freedom of Spirit who enables us to see Christ the light of the world in the world. Reflection is a kind of attention or attentiveness to the presence of Christ who is engaged in a passionate concern for the world. This kind of reflection is not passive, it is energized and animated by the life of God itself, and this life is the *missio Dei*. Attention therefore finds its origin in this mission and it is stirred as it is taken up into the life of God. Reflection therefore is a participation in God who is mission in the world. Sharing in the mission of God through the intentional practice of practical theology and theological reflection is both cultural practice and a participation in the divine life. It is lived in and indwelt.

Reflection as the Transforming Light of Christ

Participation and mediation indicate the extent to which practical theology is theological because it is 'reflection'. This means that although much of practical theology is focused on the expression of the Church, it is not necessarily theology. It is reflection, that is, the transforming freedom of the Spirit, which makes practical theology 'theology'.

---

274 Bosch, D. (1992), *Transforming Mission: Paradigm Shifts in Theology of Mission*, Maryknoll: Orbis, p. 10.

275 Barth, K. (1957), 'Theology and Mission in the Present', trans. Nigrelli, D., in Thomas, N. (ed.) (1995), *Readings in World Mission*, London: SPCK, p. 106.

The cultural study of a congregation, or the investigation of how faith develops are not in and of themselves 'theology'. Neither should it be assumed that it is the judicious inclusion of systematic theology that makes practical theology 'theology'. Practical theology is theological because it is reflection. Reflection is the mediation of and a participation in the Trinitarian life of God. Theological reflection has it origins in the light. As St Paul says, 'it is the God who said, "Let light shine out of darkness", who has shone in our hearts to give the light of the knowledge of the glory of God in the face of Jesus Christ'.[276] Theological reflection is a participation in this divine light and life. The light is the glory of God, which shines forth from the face of Christ who is the image of God. Practical theology is a cultural and academic discipline, but its energy and freedom has its origins in Christ. With unveiled faces the freedom of the Spirit is a transforming energy. The light of Christ in reflection changes us from glory into glory. Transformation, says Barth, comes from Christ who acts on us like light upon a mirror, 'we ourselves are a mirror in whom the Lord sees himself and in whom he discovers his own image, so that confronting us, he takes and uses us as a mirror and we are actually changed into his image. His glory becomes our glory and his image our image.'[277]

In reflection practical theology becomes a transforming participation in glory. We are changed through the freedom of the Spirit into the image of Christ who is the light and glory of God. The practice of theological reflection is simultaneously then a personal sanctification and glorification and a participation in the mission of God. The transformation is the gospel of God, and according to Calvin, 'the purpose of the gospel is the restoration in us of the image of God which had been cancelled by sin and that this restoration is progressive and goes on during our whole life, because God makes his glory shine in us little by little'.[278]

The freedom of the Spirit is the transforming freedom of sharing in the mission of God. This means that the cultural discipline of reflecting

---

276 2 Cor. 4.6.

277 Barth, K. (1975), *Church Dogmatics III/1* (2nd Edn), (trans. Bromiley, G.W. and Torrance, T.F) Edinburgh: T and T Clark, p. 204.

278 Calvin, J. (1964), *The Second Epistle of Paul to the Corinthians and the Epistles of Timothy, Titus and Philemon*, trans, Smail, T. A., Grand Rapids: Eerdmans, p. 50.

upon ministry is located in the flow of the Trinitarian life. Practical theology becomes the pursuit of Christ the light of the world and the image of God. This is more than a spiritual or personal sanctification because it is in and through reflection that the minister engages in the life and mission of God to the world. Faith seeking understanding is an intentional practice of participation in God who in mission is Trinity. In theological reflection practical theology is both lived in as a cultural practice and it is indwelt through a participation in the divine life and light. Reflection is transforming because it is a gradual glorification and transformation into Christ, who is the image of God. This approach to practical theology as participation and mediation means that it is reframed as a spiritual discipline.

Through the practice of reflection we are free and, with unveiled faces, taken up and transformed in the contemplation of Christ. This is what Hughes speaks of in his commentary on 2 Corinthians: 'to contemplate Him who is the Father's image is progressively to be transformed into that image. The effect of continuous beholding is that we are continuously being transformed into the "same image", that is into the likeness of Christ.'[279]

---

279 Hughes, P. (1962), *Paul's Second Epistle to the Corinthians*, NICNT, Grand Rapids: Eerdmans, p. 117.

6

Mediation

Theology could be thought of as the attempt to produce a picture of faith. Through definition and close attention to sources, it sets out to produce the perfect image of belief captured in text. The theologian might therefore be likened to a painter, for instance, the Dutch master Johannes Vermeer. Peter Webber's film *Girl with a Pearl Earring* gives an insight into the painstaking and detailed way in which the artist Vermeer worked.[280] Through the use of metaphor and analogy, like Vermeer's painting, theology tries to capture the subtle play of (divine) light on the texture of life. Theological expression can appear to be a static text, which like Vermeer's subjects, presents a perfection frozen in time. Yet this impression of theology as the attempt to produce the perfect picture or text is problematic because it tends to locate the theological as a form of static definition or abstraction.

The previous chapter argued that theology is 'theology' because it is a participation in the Trinitarian life of God. This participation is mediated in the expression of the Christian community. This means that rather than simply being a form of static definition, theology should perhaps be seen as communication. This communication is both lived in as a culture and at the same time it is indwelt by God. In communication 'theology' is animated within the community. Animation relates to a 'quickening' that gives life to the theological as it is communicated. Communities and individuals animate theology through expression and identification, and, as such, animation is a way of life. At the same time, animation relates to the way that theology is made alive (as reflection) through the freedom of the Spirit of God. So theology is animated as it is moved or circulated within the Christian community,

280 *Girl with a Pearl Earring* (2003), directed by Peter Webber.

and as it is animated it becomes 'theology', that is, a participation in transforming glory.

For the minister this reading of the theological as animation is a vital move within practical theology. It forges a connection between the everyday lived faith of the Church and of ministerial practice and reasoned reflection. Within the Christian community we participate in the animation of theology as we pray, think, debate, make decisions, preach sermons, sing songs, read the Bible, and so on. Practical theology forms a continuity with these practices because definition, however abstract, is not frozen in time like a painting. Reflection is a circulation of reasoned expression that animates theology and is theology as it is animated in and through the Spirit. Theology should therefore not be seen simply as static definition but rather as an animated communication set in motion by the participation of the Christian community. The animation of theology in the Christian community operates as mediation.

Mediation

Mediation is one of Raymond Williams's keywords, and just like culture it also has a complex lineage. In early English usage, says Williams, mediation refers to the action of an intermediary. So in Chaucer the 'mediation' of an intermediary relates to a reconciling action between two adversaries.[281] This idea of an intermediary in later use is extended to refer to the way that media enable communication across distances and can therefore be thought of as having a kind of reconciling action that brings people closer together. An example of this is the telephone. Through the medium of the telephone two people can communicate even if they are thousands of miles apart. The telephone operates as mediation because it functions as an intermediary. Media of all kinds act as intermediaries, for instance the postcard or the popular song are both mediations, as are newspapers, television and the internet. Within this understanding of mediation as an intermediary action, institutions, groups and individuals that are engaged in the production

---

281 Williams, R. (1976), *Keywords: A Vocabulary of Culture and Society*, Glasgow: Fontana.

of media are seen as agents that are engaged in shaping communication and meaning.[282] Keith Negus argues that mediation as intermediary action in popular music studies relates to the activities of individuals and organizations such as record companies, music producers, publicists and festival organizers. As intermediaries they are involved creatively in the production of music. This means that a whole range of activities and actions lie behind not only the construction of individual songs and recordings, but also the way that artists and musical genres such as country and western or hip hop are 'produced'.

Mediation as intermediary action is evident in a number of different ways in the Christian community. At a basic level mediation is clearly evident in the way that churches have adopted the communication and information technology associated with popular culture. Christian websites, radio stations, festivals and publishing exist as intermediaries communicating across distances. Mediation, however, is also found in the more traditional forms of communication in the Church such as preaching, the construction of liturgies, the parish magazine and theological publishing. Just as in the production of popular music, there are individuals, groups and institutions who are active agents engaged in shaping this kind of ecclesial expression as it is mediated. These actions circulate and move theology and set it in motion. This circulation is an animation of theological expression. The intermediary action of agents in generating a circulating theological expression becomes animated in the freedom of the Spirit. Mediation therefore is animation as it becomes a place of transforming glory. So the participation of agents in the active mediation of theology exists as a culture, but it is also a place of divine encounter.

Media actively shape expression in and through their transmission. Mediation as transmission refers to the role of media in distributing and making representation available. An example of this is the way that radio transmits or broadcasts programmes. Transmission focuses attention on the way that texts are set in motion through mediation. They move across the divide between producers and consumers, but transmission also affects the shape and construction of texts. So in mediation there are possibilities for communication but there are also

---

282 Williams, *Keywords*; Negus, K. (1996), *Popular Music in Theory: An Introduction*, Cambridge: Polity Press, pp. 67–9.

limitations. A good example of this is the pop record. Recording transformed popular music from an industry that was mainly based around the production of sheet music to one that was primarily focused on the marketing and distribution of recording artists.[283] The record transmitted the performance of a particular artist such as Elvis or Frank Sinatra beyond the live concert and into the living room and the bedroom. At the same time recording as mediation involved limitations, and these limitations shaped popular song as text and as performance. Recording technology meant that songs were limited to the capacity of the early 78 and later the 45 rpm discs. The three-minute format of the pop song largely owes its origins to these limits. So recording transmitted performance while at the same time it affected the shape of that performance. There are similar limits and conventions associated with all kinds of mediation from television formats to the design of web pages.

The practice of the Church transmits theological expression in a variety of mediated forms. The use of particular media enables the communication of faith but it also shapes expression. A good example is the use of writing and publishing to convey theological expression. Printing has been a favoured form of mediation in theological study and in the Church. In the sixteenth century advances in printing technology meant that Bibles and other theological treatises suddenly became much more widely accessible. This mediated revolution served to transmit the theology of the Reformation across Europe.[284] Since the Reformation, printing has been used to transmit theological expression, but it has also shaped that expression. Printing tends to favour the written word, and writing has a structure that is predominantly linear in form. This means that the writer must shape his or her thought as a structured and progressive argument. Just as one word must follow another as it is written, so must one idea follow on from the one before. The relationship between the written word, printing and theological reasoning has both mediated and limited expression. The structure of a written theological book is quite different to a piece of choral music, for instance, where several texts might be layered over one another and shaped by different singers into a harmony. In addition to the interweaving of

---

283 See Shuker, R. (1994), *Understanding Popular Music*, London: Routledge.
284 See Lindberg, C. (1996), *The European Reformations*, Oxford: Blackwell.

voices and lyrics choral pieces are generally accompanied by some form of musical instrumentation. This adds a further perceptual complexity and layer of meaning to the expression. Choral music is generally performed in the context of an act of worship. Here again there is a difference between written theological expression and the experience of an act of worship where music, architecture, words, colour, smell and the physical presence of people gathered together produce a complex textual interplay. The difference between theological expression in written texts and in choral music, and worship more generally, illustrates the way that writing and publishing have acted to shape academic theology into a particular form. Mediation creates possibilities, but as it does so it also limits the form that expression might take. These limitations act on the possibilities of texts as a form as they are communicated.

The transmission of theological expression is also an animation. Animation relates to the way that through mediation expression is set in motion. The media enable and extend ecclesial communication. Through the use of media theological expression moves and circulates as it is transmitted between people and across distances. Transmission moves theology, and as it is moved it is quickened and brought to life. Transmission operates as communication and culture, but it is also a place of encounter. Communion is mediated in and through the circulation of expression. So mediation expresses the way that theology as it is animated mediates participation in God. The media therefore operate as an active agent in this transmission not simply in the circulation of expression but also in determining its shape.

Communication is made by people and so mediation relates to the social relationships that act to condition and shape communication. For Negus this kind of mediation is seen in the way that popular music is consumed and the cultures that fans build around the music. [285] Young people act as mediators as they make use of songs and artists in their daily lives. Practices such as using pictures of bands to decorate a bedroom, or the selection of music to download as a mix on their mobile phone or MP3 player, mean that young people are active agents in relation to popular culture. These kinds of choices form patterns of similarity and difference and they therefore function as a source for

---

285 Negus, K. (1996), *Popular Music in Theory: An Introduction*, Cambridge: Polity Press, pp. 67–9.

identity construction. It is for this reason that youth cultures are often very closely identified with styles of music as well as with fashion and behaviour. Through consumption these various elements are mediated as a distinctive identity.

As well as acting as mediation through the practices associated with consumption social relationships are also a significant factor in the production of popular culture. Artists of all kinds, be they musicians, film makers or writers, are creative within a social environment. So the experience of urban life or a family upbringing, for instance, might be seen as an influence on an artist's work. The mediation of social relationships in production is widely recognized, for instance, in the way that films are made through a collaboration between people working together. An example of this kind of mediation through social relationships can be seen therefore in the creative dynamic between a film director and an actor, or a cinematographer and an editor. In these various ways mediation within social relationships can be seen as adding a particular quality or a 'feel' to a film.

Within the Christian community this social dimension to faith and its communication is widely accepted and understood. The 'fellowship' of Christians, for example, is generally seen as a vital source of strength and encouragement. So gathering for worship or prayer and Bible study is a form of mediation. This is because it is through these kinds of communal practices that the Church mediates faith. This form of mediation it should be noted is also an animation that is both cultural and spiritual. We live among and in the Christian community while at the same time experiencing these social relationships as being divinely charged. The presence of the Spirit in the Church is animated in and through the mediation of social relationships.

Mediation and Presence

The communication of the Church operates as a series of different mediations. Mediation therefore presents as culture, but it is also a participation in the Trinitarian life of God. Through mediation ecclesial life is extended beyond the local congregation and becomes more fluid. Mediation animates the theological, quickening it as it sets it in motion.

This mediation of the divine life in the communication of the Church cannot be assumed. The Church cannot summon the divine presence. Both mediation and participation imply that there is a significant place for human agency in the circulation of 'theology', but this action does not construct, instruct or necessitate encounter with God. Mediation becomes a transforming encounter as it is made so by the Spirit of freedom. This approach to mediation rests on a personal, dynamic, fluid and intentional presence of God. Reflected glory is the personal presence of God mediated in the Son who is the image of God. This understanding of the personal presence of God in mediation is distinct from the idea of omnipresence. Omnipresence suggests that God is always and everywhere near. Omnipresence situates mediation as participation in the divine life because that life is in all things. Fruitful as omnipresence might be, it introduces a mechanistic and inevitable dimension into mediation. Omnipresence downplays the relational, the intimate and the particular. This approach to mediation represents glory as background lighting rather than the ray of sunlight, it is more like the hum of the bass amp as opposed to the punchy riff. There are similar limitations in dealing with mediation through a theology of creation. Such a theology might view the world and human making as aspects of a creation that is sustained within and around by the Spirit. This creation emphasis may have a place in theological expression, but it, like omnipresence, also serves to downplay the relational and personal presence of God in mediation.

Rather than locate mediation within ideas of omnipresence or in a theology of creation, the relational and personal presence of God might be seen as 'epiphany'. Epiphany emphasizes revealing moments. In epiphany God is intentionally and personally present in mediation. Epiphany speaks of the way that divine freedom is exercised in participation. This notion of epiphany as the freedom of God has a resonance with Barth's discussion of the proclamation of the Church in the opening volume of the *Church Dogmatics*.[286] For Barth the Church has a commission to engage in talk about God. Preaching and the sacraments are distinctive as proclamation because of this commission.

---

286 I accept that this may well be seen as a reading that is against the grain of Barth's general approach to culture.

The distinctiveness of proclamation comes from the Word of God.[287] Preaching is not necessarily proclamation, it must 'ever and again' become so. It is this becoming which makes the Church the Church.[288] Proclamation is not distinctive because of a particular message or set of values. God's Word is the content of proclamation and as such it becomes an object for human study, but as proclamation it can never be objectified. In proclamation it 'presents and places itself as an object over and against us'.[289] As Barth puts it, 'We have it as it gives itself to us.'[290] This is an event of revelation. A revealing or, as I prefer it in the context of the present discussion, an 'epiphany'. In this encounter the humanity of those who proclaim, says Barth, is not cast aside, because proclamation becomes itself as an event among other human events and it can be read on this level. As Christ became a true man and his humanity continues throughout eternity, proclamation exists as a human acting and making. Yet there is a new 'robe of righteousness thrown over it and its earthly character takes on another kind of event'. Real proclamation is an event where human talk about God becomes a place where God speaks about himself.[291] Talk about God rests on the canon of scripture, but scripture, like the proclamation of the Church, is itself a human recollection of revelation.[292] The Bible is the means by which the Church remembers past revelation and is 'called to an expectation of His future revelation and is thus summoned and guided to proclamation and empowered for it'.[293] Thus for Barth both proclamation and scripture are conditioned by the Word of God revealed. This is what is meant by God with us.[294] Revelation as a revealing is conditioned by the act of revelation. What this means, says Barth, is that, 'Revelation in fact does not differ from the person of Jesus Christ nor from the revelation accomplished in him.'[295] By talking of revelation we

287 Barth, K. (1975), *Church Dogmatics* I/1 (2nd edn), trans. Bromiley, G. W. and Torrance, T. F., Edinburgh: T&T Clark, p. 47.

288 Barth, *CD* I/1, p. 88.

289 Barth, *CD* I/1, p. 91.

290 Barth, *CD* I/1, p. 92.

291 Barth, *CD* I/1, p. 95.

292 Barth, *CD* I/1, p. 102.

293 Barth, *CD* I/1, p. 111.

294 Barth, *CD* I/1, p. 116.

295 Barth, *CD* I/1, p. 119.

inevitably speak therefore of the God who was made flesh and dwelt among us. This takes us to the Trinity. The Word made flesh is the will of the Father and the sending of the Son and the Spirit. It is the knowledge of God from God and of 'light in light'.[296] It is God who reveals God's self. [297] So God's speaking is not to be distinguished from God. For Barth revelation is therefore a personal address that confronts humanity but, and this is the crucial point, the Word of God is always 'mediated' in the proclamation of the Church. So if the Word of God is God's self, then scripture and the preaching of the Church are not to be taken as self-evidently and inevitably revelation. Rather they become so as an event, as a free act of God's grace. It is in this freedom and through grace that God reveals himself as the Lord.[298]

Barth's treatment of revelation connects mediation with a Christologically articulated Trinitarian theology. The preaching of the Church is acknowledged as mediation. It is human speech and therefore cultural. At the same time it is a place where God reveals God's self. God's revelation is an event, an act received in faith. Revelation is not inevitable. It is not negotiated or deduced from a specific content of what has been revealed in scripture or in past proclamation. Revelation is dynamic and personal, and as such it is focused in Jesus Christ and in the reconciliation he brings.

For Barth the specific calling of the Church to proclamation is located in preaching and the sacraments. I want to suggest that this ecclesial focus is extended and made more fluid by mediation. Mediation draws attention to the nature and complexity of communication in the Christian community. In this much wider understanding of mediation there is an animation or a quickening as the free God becomes present. This is what is meant by epiphany. Epiphanies are mediated through culture, but they are located in God's self. Revelation is Trinitarian and its content is Jesus Christ. God's freedom to be present is a Trinitarian event mediated in and through the communication of the Church.

---

296 Barth, *CD* I/1, p. 119.
297 Barth, *CD* I/1, p. 296.
298 Barth, *CD* I/1, p. 306.

Contemplation

Epiphany emphasizes the personal and intentional presence of God in the intimacy of encounter, but it is in danger of suggesting that communion is momentary or episodic in nature. To balance this tendency alongside epiphany I want to introduce the idea of contemplation or attention. Contemplation articulates mediation with participation in a way that foregrounds agency. In epiphany God is free. Yet epiphany is mediated by the agency of individuals and communities through the practice of disciplines of contemplation or attention. This notion of contemplation can be explored in more detail through a discussion of the link that Athanasius makes between attention, salvation and the image of God in humanity.

For Athanasius the image of God rests on the creative imprint of the Word on every human being. Humanity, through the creative work of the Word, shares with the Word the same reason which shaped the world.[299] But the image of God, says Athanasius, is not a 'natural' or inherent gift, rather the divine imprint must always be maintained and sustained. It is only through a continual attention to, and contemplation of, the Word that the image is kept alive. 'By nature of course man is mortal, since he was made from nothing, but he bears also the likeness of him who is and if he preserves that likeness through constant contemplation then his nature is deprived of its power and remains incorrupt.'[300]

With corruption this constant contemplation was interrupted and humanity becomes 'bereft of grace'.[301] For Athanasius mortality is reinforced through a turning of attention from things that are eternal to those that are corruptible. The shift of attention towards the corruptible leads in turn to corruption, and the effects of mortality are unchecked by grace.[302] It is for the restoration and rescue of humanity that the Word 'entered the world'. The Word had of course not been far from the world, says Athanasius, for 'no part of creation had ever been without Him who, while ever abiding in union with the Father,

---

299 Athanasius (1944), *St Athanasius on the Incarnation*, translated by a religious of CSMV, London: Mowbray.
300 Athanasius, *Incarnation*, p. 30.
301 Athanasius, *Incarnation*, p. 33.
302 Athanasius, *Incarnation*, p. 33.

yet fills all things that are'.[303] Now, however, the Word enters the world in a new way and he 'stoops to our level in His love and Self-revealing to us'.[304] The recreation of the image of God in humanity required that death and corruption be addressed. Redemption, for Athanasius, operates first as a renewal of mortality through the Word, which takes our flesh upon himself. Like a king entering a city, his glory transforms it from within.[305] Second, through his death and resurrection, death and corruption are 'utterly abolished'.[306] The restoration of the image enables a renewal of attention and contemplation. This contemplation is itself aided by the incarnation of the Word. The saviour of the world seeing that people were focused on 'sensible things' becomes himself an object for the senses.[307]

> There were thus two things which the Saviour did for us by becoming Man. He banished death from us and made us anew; and, invisible and imperceptible as in himself he is, he became visible through his works and revealed himself as the Word of the Father, the Ruler and King of the whole creation.[308]

Recreated in and through the incarnation, death and resurrection of the Word of God, the restoration of humanity is once again linked to the sustaining dynamic of contemplation. The visibility of the Word enables the dynamic of attention to recommence in the renewed creature. Restoration and contemplation lead to participation in the divine. The incarnation therefore operates at a number of levels to bring unity between humanity and divinity. 'For he was made man that we might be made God; and he manifested himself by a body that we might receive the idea of the unseen Father; and he endured the insolence of men that we might inherit immortality.'[309]

---

303 Athanasius, *Incarnation*, p. 33.
304 Athanasius, *Incarnation*, p. 33.
305 Athanasius, *Incarnation*, pp. 35ff.
306 Athanasius, *Incarnation*, p. 49.
307 Athanasius, *Incarnation*, p. 44.
308 Athanasius, *Incarnation*, p. 45.
309 Athanasius (1891), *Incarnation of the Word*, in *A Select Library of the Nicene and Post-Nicene Fathers of the Christian Church*, ed. Schaff, P., Second Series, vol. 4: *St Athanasius: Select Works and Letters*, Oxford: Parker, p. 65.

Mediation and Attention

Mediation operates as animation that sets 'theology' in motion. Participation in the circulation of theological expression is a mediation of attention and contemplation. The discipline of contemplative prayer linked to the 'Jesus Prayer' illustrates this idea of mediation as contemplation. This form of prayer uses the phrase 'Lord Jesus Christ, Son of God, have mercy on me.' Through the repetition of the phrases and practices, such as the regulation of breathing, the prayer structures a discipline of attention.[310] Praying the Jesus Prayer sets in motion this particular theological expression. Participation in this kind of prayer requires an active moving of the words in a series of repetitions either spoken out loud or in the mind. This discipline in turn mediates the divine presence. The prayer is a practice of contemplation because it is focused on engendering an attention on Christ that is continuous. Contemplation, however, is mediated within the words of the prayer as they are animated or set in motion. So the individual is an active agent in this practice.

The animation of 'theology' seen in the Jesus Prayer can be extended to the wider communicative practices of the Christian community. In mediation attention and contemplation are situated in the participation in the circulation of 'theology'. Individuals and communities are therefore active agents in the animation of 'theology'. Attention involves a discipline of continual participation. Mediation extends the ecclesial context of this circulation. So we can see that, set alongside the sacraments and the preaching of the word, there are a whole raft of communicative practices and texts that are animated through mediation. As we have seen, participation is framed through the understanding of mediation as intermediary action, transmission and social relations. This means that attention and contemplation should be seen as relating to the agency of individuals and institutions in productive processes. It also relates to the transmission of theological expression in representation. The expression (of theology) is therefore a form of attention because it is an active participation in circulation. Similarly the way that communities form their sense of self around practices such as worship is also a participation in the mediation and animation

---

310 For more on the Jesus Prayer see Sjogren, P. (1975), *The Jesus Prayer*, trans. Linton, S., London: SPCK.

of 'theology'. Theological texts operate as mediation in a dynamic of circulation between production and consumption. As such they are animated as they are circulated. It is in this circulation that they become a mediation of contemplation. This idea of a mediation as circulation does not just apply to practices such as worship or prayer. The discipline of practical theology also forms a part of this communicative flow. Through its productive processes and the ways in which these find a location in the missional life of communities practical theology is seen to be participation, animation and attention.

Theological Capital

Mediation and attention are situated in communities in a dynamic relationship with existing knowledge, practice and custom. This existing knowledge forms a kind of theological capital. The idea of theological capital is significant because it foregrounds what people bring to the circulation of expression. Theological capital operates as a form of mediation situating expression in a way of life. So theological capital offers an orientation and a shape to attention and the circulation of expression.[311]

Through my involvement in Christian youth work I realized that there were important differences between young people who had grown up inside the Church and those who had not. The Church young people seemed to be able to relate quite easily to a Bible passage or the lyrics of a worship song. Through their time in Sunday school, and from their parents, they had developed not only specific knowledge but also a framework that allowed them to interact with the kind of things we were doing in the youth work. For young people from outside Christian families this kind of interaction proved to be much more difficult. They could struggle to make sense of the lyrics of songs, and the Bible was often hard going and occasionally inaccessible to them. The young people from Christian families had developed a theological capital that enabled them to manoeuvre and position their own lives in relation to theological expression. This capital operated as a form

---

311 This idea of theological capital is adapted from Pierre Bourdieu's theory of practice. For more on the theory of practice see Chapter 10.

of mediation shaping how theology is situated in a way of life. The absence of theological capital on the other hand meant that the young people from outside of the Church often found it hard to make sense of themselves in relation to the things we were doing as youth workers. So absence of theological capital restricted their ability to interact with the expression of theology.

Theological capital results from the way that in mediation 'theology' is not only circulated, it is also internalized. Internalized theological expression is an animating and transformative force. Participation and attention cannot then be reduced to attendance at worship or the repetition of prayers. The circulation of expression animates the theological, but this is articulated as it is made part of a way of life. Capital shapes identity, and as part of identity it acts to mediate circulation. Participation generates theological capital. It is by sharing in the circulation of expression that individuals internalize 'theology'. This form of meaning-making and identity formation is a kind of necessary theological work. Animating and being animated by the theological has a transforming impact on believers and communities. Capital is developed in the context of an active sharing in the communication of the Church. At the same time theological capital enables this participation and forms a part of the interpretative and creative resource in expression. Capital is therefore related to the communicative practices of particular sites. So individuals may gain theological capital by attending a Christian event such as Greenbelt or a study programme. Capital can also be generated by joining a church music group or listening to worship music in the car on the way to work. Participation in the circulation of expression generates theological capital, but it also presupposes the Christian community. The Christian festival and the worship CD are ways in which mediation extends and makes more fluid the communication of the contemporary Church. These intermediary actions expand and liquify the sites where capital might be generated and used. So the fluid nature of mediation circulates theological expression way beyond the local congregation or parish. Theological capital should not be regarded solely as an internalized form of knowledge or a disposition. Theological capital is a mediation of the divine life in the individual. It is an animation or quickening of the believer.

Practical Theology Without Guarantees

Throughout this discussion there have been constant references to mediation as a participation in the divine life. This pattern of theological expression and communion with God, as a lived-in culture or way of life that is also indwelt through the freedom of the Spirit, has been a feature of the argument so far. Participation has been presented as a sharing in the life of the Trinity. So the being of God, as Father, Son and Holy Spirit, structures mediation as it is in turn mediated in the cultural. This structuring for Barth and for Athanasius is Christologically focused. Revelation, for Barth, is the revelation of the Word, just as contemplation for Athanasius is a continual attention to the Word revealed through the incarnation. This Christological pattern in mediation links to the previous discussion of reflection as a participation in divine glory, since it is in the face of Christ that the light shines; and the image reproduced through reflection is that of the Son who is the image of the Father. This theological patterning sets a framework within which mediation can be understood but it also raises the question of normativity and evaluation. Part of the task of practical theology relates to a critical judgement of the expression of the Church. The Trinitarian patterning in participation appears to promise a clear and coherent theological position from which to make these kinds of evaluative judgements.

There are two ways in which evaluation and normativity have traditionally been exercised in the Christian community. The first way has been through definition and written doctrinal formulation and the second has been through institution and authorized ministry. As we have seen, mediation sets both doctrine and the institution of the Church in a dynamic and fluid interplay of communication. It is not so much that these frameworks are negated by mediation, rather that they must be seen to operate as part of a more complex confused and yet continuous whole. Theology is 'theology' because it is a participation in God, and so mediation has a Trinitarian structure. Yet this patterning must be discerned in and by means of a reflective practice that is itself cultural. So mediation serves to 'muddy the waters' and produce a practical theology that is without guarantees.

7

Communion and Mediation

So far theology has been presented as participation and mediation. This theological discussion, concerning the relationship between theology and the cultural, if it is to be convincing and indeed true to itself, must be seen to be operative (or animated) in the practice and expression of the Church. Such a connection, I want to suggest, is found in the Eucharist. When I first became a Christian, the Church that I attended called the Eucharist 'Communion'. Communion is rich in connotation. It speaks of the fellowship of believers joined in a communion as they worship together. This communion extends beyond the congregation to the wider Church. Thus the worldwide Anglican Church refers to itself as a communion. At the same time we were told as we went through our confirmation preparation that we were being prepared to 'make our first communion'. This is an interesting term. The communion spoken of is clearly concerned with intimacy. We were being prepared for an encounter with God that was mediated in the taking of bread and wine, but it is also telling that this intimacy was presented as something that we would be 'making'. We were to be active agents participating in this encounter. In the act of communion we were sharing in the divine mystery – a real presence. So in this simple and rather everyday expression there is contained all that has so far been argued. In the lived practice of the Church communion operates as both participation and mediation.

The Eucharist also serves as a point at which the discussion of mediation and participation can be brought together with the way of seeing drawn from cultural studies. Communion is 'made' in a variety of ways. There are processes of production that are active in constructing the Eucharist as liturgy and as practice. These productive processes produce the Eucharist as liturgical texts. Each text is a representation, but liturgy must also be enacted if it is to be animated in the life of the community. Liturgical performance produces through articulation, that is, the joining together of hymns, ritual, music, and so on, a representation or an expression of faith. So the Eucharist is produced as representation in performance. Performance sets theology in motion as it mediates encounter with God. Encounter, however, is mediated in and through human relations. The Christian community actively participates in the performance of the eucharistic representation and as it does so it shapes its identity. So communion can be read as mediation and participation that is produced, represented and consumed.

Drawing upon ideas of production, representation and consumption, the Eucharist is an appropriate place to explore the connection between mediation and participation and the lived expression of the Christian community. At the same time communion is also a key point of departure for practical theology because it is generally regarded as the central act of Christian worship.[312] This situates the Eucharist at an important and strategic point in this discussion. Communion lies at the heart of Christian theology. By showing how participation and mediation connect to this practice I want to advance the much wider argument concerning the nature of theology and the implications of this for the shape of practical theology.

The Performance of Doctrine

At the heart of the celebration of the Eucharist lies a Pauline text taken from the First Letter to the Corinthians:

> For I received from the Lord what I also handed on to you, that the Lord Jesus on the night when he was betrayed took a loaf of bread and when he had given thanks, he broke it and said. 'This is my body that is for you. Do this in remembrance of me.' In the same way he took the cup also after supper, saying, 'This cup is the new covenant in my blood. Do this as often as you drink it, in remembrance of me.' For as often as you eat this bread and drink the cup, you proclaim the Lord's death until he comes.[313]

312 The one exception to this may be the Salvation Army.
313 1 Cor. 11.23–6.

This text has a setting within a biblical and Pauline context but it also has a place in the worship of the Church. A consideration of the contemporary meaning of this text is therefore not limited to the area of biblical studies. Its significance is also related to the way that the Christian community has used it as part of eucharistic worship. Framed as the 'narrative of institution' this biblical text has a central place in eucharistic worship in the majority of liturgical traditions. The question of the meaning in relation to this text is therefore not wholly expressed or encompassed by an examination of its original setting or biblical context. Any exploration of the text must also find a way to consider how it has contributed to Christian identity, expression, worship and so on.

In the liturgy the text is enacted, re-enacted or performed. It is important to understand that performance is inherent in the text itself, since here the Christian community is commanded, 'Do this is remembrance of me.' To speak of performance therefore is to run with the grain of the biblical text. The performance of the text in worship is part of its setting in the Pauline letter just as it is in the liturgical practice of the Church. The text is performed in the liturgy. It is therefore part of its sense that this text is to be embodied. In the Eucharist this text is performed and it becomes an enacted or embodied theology. When a Christian community performs the liturgy these words become 'lived in' and a way of life. At the same time the performance of the liturgy is also 'indwelt', that is, it becomes a place of divine revelation and encounter. To be lived in and indwelt this biblical text needs to be performed. Moreover, to speak of the 'lived-in-ness' of the Eucharist does not preclude talk of 'indwelt-ness', since in performance these two are interdependent. Performance as embodied theology is situated in particular communities, liturgical rites and historical contexts. The question of meaning in relation to this biblical text is thus articulated by performance. This means that if we want to explore the question of meaning in relation to the performance of this text in the Eucharist we need to find ways of seeing which take account of the complexities of community life, social context and liturgical formulation and expression. Such an enterprise, it should be stressed, does not necessarily reduce the theological to the cultural because as we have already noted, it is of the nature of the Eucharist that it is a text in performance, that is, it is both lived in and indwelt. To speak of one therefore is to also speak of the other.

The Eucharist is performed or set in motion through a series of mediations. There are the intermediary actions of individuals and institutions engaged in the production of liturgy and theology within ecclesial traditions. These actions produce texts that 'transmit' theological representation. Texts exist both as written liturgies and as representation that circulates and is animated by performance. Finally there is the mediation that operates within the Christian community through the relationship between individual and communal identity and texts that are set in motion in performance. How mediation operates in the Eucharist will therefore be explored through the three phases of production, representation and audience drawn from the cultural circuit.

The Production of the Eucharist

The Eucharist has been produced within the Christian community through a long process of liturgical development. In this production there has been an interaction between liturgical scholars, ecclesial bodies and the production of particular liturgies. An account of the production of the Eucharist might therefore include the key role of individuals such as Dom Gregory Dix or Gabriel Herbert in liturgical reform during the twentieth century, or a discussion of the role of the Anglican Liturgical Commission and its revision of the Prayer book culminating in the publication of *Common Worship*.[314] Alongside this kind of production we can place the various debates concerning the theology of the eucharistic. These theological debates might include an account of the on-going discussion about the presence of Christ in the eucharistic elements and the various doctrinal formulations adopted by different churches. Production therefore relates to the way that individuals and institutions have acted to try to shape meaning in eucharistic performance. The text is produced because, like 'Shine, Jesus, shine', it has been 'inscribed' or encoded in the various liturgical texts. These liturgical texts are produced within ecclesial and theological

---

314 Archbishops' Council (2000), *Common Worship*, London: Church House Publishing.

traditions. In liturgical studies it is common for these traditions to be explored to reveal layers of inscribed or intended meaning.

Production does not relate solely to the way that traditions have produced liturgical texts: there are also social aspects in production. Communities and individuals are 'produced' as they participate in the circulation and creation of specific traditions. An example of this is the way that individuals may be shaped by a tradition such as Anglo-Catholicism. The culture of priesthood is passed on within this tradition not simply through theological texts but also through formation. Formation within Anglo-Catholicism is a social process whereby individuals are shaped in their sense of self and their understanding of the meaning of the Eucharist.[315] Formation therefore can be seen as a kind of production in that it not only trains and shapes individuals as priests, it also produces a particular understanding of the eucharistic performance. For a while I was a member of the congregation in a Church that had strong links to the Anglo-Catholic theological college, St Stephen's House. It was interesting to observe the way that the the St Stephen's House ordinands seemed to adopt a particular style in relation to the Eucharist. This style was so marked that it was easy to spot ordinands in the congregation by the way they behaved. For instance during the eucharistic prayer, for some reason, they would stand when everyone else in church sat or knelt.

If we are to discuss how a text like 1 Cor. 11.23–6 is produced we will need to adopt a variety of methods of enquiry as part of practical theology. These may be largely familiar to the theologian. They involve the examination of theological texts, ecclesial formulations and historical records, among other things. The discussion of particular liturgies and liturgical theologies will be required to demonstrate changes in liturgical practice. Production, however, might also involve a consideration of sociological data. An examination of how priestly formation shapes eucharistic performance, for example, would involve the use of more social-scientific methods of enquiry.

---

315 For more on the development of a culture within Anglo-Catholicism, see Shelton Reed, J. (1996), *Glorious Battle: The Cultural Politics of Victorian Anglo-Catholicism*, London: Tufton Books.

Representation and the Eucharist

A discussion of production does not of itself yield a full account of the Eucharist. One of the reasons for this is that while production inscribes meaning, this meaning is not necessarily fixed through productive processes. This means that while it is important for practical theology to interact with more traditional forms of systematic, doctrinal or liturgical theology because they are ways in which meaning is inscribed in texts, it is also necessary to examine how produced and inscribed expression is performed. Inscribed or produced meaning shifts in performance through representation. One way of illustrating how the performance of the Eucharist shifts through representation is seen in the recent Anglican experience of ordaining women to the priesthood. A woman priest robed and celebrating at the altar is a particular representation. In contrast perhaps we can think of the symbolism of a circle of robed male priests around the altar concelebrating. While the liturgy, and large elements of the ritual, may be exactly the same, the difference in celebrants and style of celebration allows for a complex and perhaps contrasting range of connotations.

Performance therefore implies a particular enactment. Each enactment involves representation. Representation articulates inscribed meaning by linking it to a range of complex signifiers. Complexity or inter-textuality is a characteristic of every eucharistic performance. For while there may be a consistency in many of the elements of the liturgy it is also usual for individual eucharistic celebrations to involve a changing mix of hymns, prayers, sermon, and so on. Church practice thereby habitually creates a rich cocktail of interactions and interconnections. An interesting example of this is the way that contemporary forms of alternative worship have used visual imagery and a range of popular styles of music to self-consciously create inter-textual interactions between traditional liturgy and popular culture. An example of this would be the use of the track 'Firestarter' by the band The Prodigy used during a worship service. The track could be played at ear-bursting volume as the backing to a eucharistic prayer from the Anglican *Common Worship*, which is yelled over the top of the music. To the song and words of the liturgy a visual element might be added by perhaps using a video loop of one of the fight scenes from the movie

The Matrix projected behind the altar as the Eucharist is celebrated. The music, particularly its volume, the vocal delivery of the words of the liturgy, combined with the scenes from the movie form a rich symbolic environment.

While it is probably the case that this Eucharist is the liturgical equivalent to Hebdige's 'semiotic guerrilla warfare', such a worship event illustrates how articulation in representation and performance repositions meaning in ways that are subversive of produced meaning.[316] This kind of practice is a contemporary, and perhaps extreme, example of eucharistic performance but it serves to demonstrate how representation articulates inscribed meaning in performance. In performance meaning shifts as the elements of worship interact and inform each other.

Once again it is worth repeating the point that a consideration of representation does not necessarily entail the reduction of the theological to the cultural. The performance of the Eucharist is assumed in the Pauline narrative of institution, as it is also generic to liturgical scholarship, ecclesial formulation, and theological and doctrinal tradition. The performance of doctrine means that it is lived in as it is also indwelt. The point is that a consideration of representation is required if we are to be able to explore the way that doctrine is performed and mediated by performance. The performance of the Eucharist therefore needs to be interpreted in a way that accounts for the complexity and multilayered nature of representation, as well as the inscribed meanings familiar from the tradition. This means that in order to read the complex way that representation articulates meaning we will need to adopt methods of enquiry that take account of the inter-textual and symbolic play of performance. So practical theology will need to develop appropriate ways of reading the semiotics of worship. It will entail a theological engagement with methodologies drawn from musicology, ritual studies, discourse and content analysis and so on. These will not replace the more traditional forms of theological enquiry associated with production, rather they are made use of to develop a more complex and layered reading of performance.

---

316 Hebdige, D. (1979), *Subculture: The Meaning of Style*, London: Methuen; citing Umberto Eco. Hebdige is discussed in more detail in Part 3.

Consuming the Eucharist

Consumption or audience relates to the way that individuals and groups make use of cultural products. It focuses upon the way that identities are shaped in relation to representation and the inscribed meanings of cultural production. For our purposes consumption recognizes the extent to which questions of meaning are not limited to an investigation of theological debates or liturgical formulation and revision. Neither is it the case that meaning can be read directly or solely from worship as a performed text. When we consider the Eucharist there is always the question of the congregation and how they shape, and are shaped by, participation in the performance of the Eucharist. There is a dynamic interaction between the produced meaning of the Eucharist, the performance of the Eucharist as representation, and the interaction of individuals and groups with these meanings and how they take them up and make use of them. Here again any account of individual and communal agency in relation to the Eucharist will be complex and multilayered. There is no straight path between what is produced, or what is represented, and the way that these are received and made sense of by those in the congregation. An illustration of this is my own experience of preaching in church.

On more than one occasion after I have preached, I have been approached by an enthusiastic parishioner who is at pains to share with me how much they agreed with, or were moved by, my sermon. Unfortunately when they go into more detail I have been more than a little embarrassed to find out that they are talking about something I haven't said, or even worse, they are congratulating me because they very much agree with what I said, but they have misheard and I actually said the opposite. As I have found to my cost, meaning is not fixed by representation, despite the best efforts of the preacher!

Meaning in the Eucharist through performance finds a place in the lived world of individuals and groups. This means that if we want to explore fully questions of meaning and significance in relation to the Eucharist we need to find ways to examine the way that meaning shifts as it is taken up and transformed by, and transforms, those in the congregation. Such an exploration needs to open up the way that meaning is circulated through representation indirectly. For instance the indirect nature of consumption is revealed by the way that congregations 'make do'. Making do refers to the way individuals use hymns, liturgies, sermons, and so on, which may not be the best or the most contextually appropriate, but despite this they are still able to 'find a way' to encounter God and shape a Christian identity. To draw on my own experience again, as a teenager I was first introduced to the Christian faith in a very formal and traditional Anglican Church. Although my musical tastes were for bands like Led Zeppelin and Black Sabbath, at church I was introduced to the English choral tradition. I must confess, I hated it, mainly for what I saw as its pretence, but somehow I made do. I found a way to develop my faith. This kind of making do is replicated in churches around the country. Parishioners know that the vicar is not the greatest preacher in the world, or that the organist is not as dexterous or adventurous as she once was, but somehow we find a way.

In relation to the Eucharist a consideration of audience can often serve to complicate questions of meaning. A good example of this is the experience of many Anglican young people who find getting out of the pew and walking to the altar to receive the eucharistic elements to be something of an embarrassment. At the level of representation and production, receiving the communion at the altar is often related to sharing of the 'one cup'. So the inscribed meaning speaks of a theology of unity. In performance, however, 'unity' can be contradicted. Rather than sharing in this ecclesial unity, some young people, especially those in early adolescence, find that the Eucharist makes them feel uncomfortable and ill at ease. The main reason for this is that they perceive that they are on display as they stand up and walk to the altar, and this makes them feel self-conscious and uncomfortable. The experience of these young people shifts the meaning away from the intentions of the tradition, and away from the theological representation of the rite, and relocates it in another and largely counterproductive place. This kind of example shows how in performance meaning can be a slippery concept to pin down.

An enquiry into what individuals make of the performance of doctrine may reveal a further level of complexity. Individual and indeed congregational belief and practice may be more intuitive and responsive than 'produced' theology. An example of this is seen in the way that individuals may hold contradictory or inconsistent theological positions on a range of themes, for example, evangelical Christians when asked about their view of biblical authority will most probably respond with some form of theory of biblical inerrancy and be very clear that their faith is fundamentally based on a biblical framework. When their spiritual practice is examined, however, it may well be the case that they rarely if ever read the Bible. This means that for instance among evangelical students, while they may be very insistent on the importance of doctrine and on the authority of the Bible, their actual knowledge of the Bible may in fact be very limited. These anomalies indicate the extent to which questions of meaning in production and representation are complicated as they are articulated through congregational and individual agency.

Again it needs to be emphasized that a consideration of meaning as it is lived in and made use of by congregations does not necessarily mean a reduction of the theological to the cultural. There is a symbiotic relationship between the produced meanings of theological discussion and liturgical formulation and the way that they are articulated through representation. The consideration of how these produced and represented meanings are lived in and how this lived-in culture in turn shapes and situates the theological is necessary to a full description of the Eucharist as performance. Here again, as with production and representation, a range of research methodologies are required by practical theology in order that it may analyse and explore meaning as it is lived in. These would include ethnographic methodologies, participant observation, structured and semi-structured interviews, and reflexive methodologies such as autobiography, narrative congregational studies, and so on.

Production, Text, Audience: General Approaches

In media/cultural studies the pattern of production, text and audience is used to develop a complex and multifaceted approach to cultural understanding. Each area of analysis is seen as being complementary to the other. It is accepted that studies may focus on aspects of production and the culture industry, or representation, or audience reception, but it is also recognized that a full account of any aspect of popular culture requires some consideration of each of the other areas. For practical theology this means, for instance, that a discussion of how individuals and congregations shape identities around the perform-ance of the Eucharist needs to take account of the interplay between communal and social reality and the specifics of representation as it is produced and as it is performed. Thus Baptist eucharistic identity may be shaped by the way that the ritual is performed and the way that the tradition has developed through theological debate. Baptist con-gregations, however, also produce and represent. They produce as they participate in the performance of the Eucharist. Production therefore relates to the way that they identify themselves with the eucharistic act in performance. Participation in performance, however, can also be read as a form of representation. Congregations mediate Baptist eucharistic identity. So individuals are socialized into Baptist practice not simply through the words and actions of the liturgy (and the tra-dition out of which these are formed) but also through worshipping with the congregation. In this way congregations can be seen to both produce and represent as they are actively participating.

A consideration of the interrelationship between production, rep-resentation and consumption is particularly important when it comes to questions of evaluation and critique. Failure to take account of the range of issues at stake when dealing with cultural expression can lead to problematic conclusions. An interesting example can be seen in the way that some conservative Christian commentators have in the past condemned heavy metal music and artists such as Ozzy Osbourne and especially his original band Black Sabbath because of the Satanic ref-erences in their songs. When Ozzy's music, and particularly the early Black Sabbath recordings, are examined, there clearly is an emphasis upon the occult. Research into audiences, however, seems to imply that the occult lyrics in heavy metal music are more likely to resonate with issues of rebellion and masculinity rather than any specifically reli-gious inclinations among teenage boys.[317] A further moderating factor relates to Ozzy Osbourne's repeated denial that he or the band had any

---

317 See Walser, R. (1993), *Running with the Devil: Power, Gender and Madness in Heavy Metal Music*, New England: Wesleyan University Press.

interest in the occult.[318] What this means is that the occult aspects of this music operate almost entirely at the level of representation. They form a part of the act rather than a part of the lived reality of the band or their audience. So the symbolic function of the Satanism in heavy metal music operates in a way that is possibly more akin to the use of the occult by Shakespeare in a play such as *The Tempest*. In other words the occult forms part of the artistic context in which audiences and artists are working symbolically with a range of issues and concerns. When theological commentators focus on representation to the exclusion of production and consumption they often fail to understand fully what is actually happening when bands perform or audiences listen to this kind of music. Moreover, in concentrating on the occult elements in the songs they miss the important theological issues which are at play in questions of masculinity, sexuality and rebellion, among some young people. A similar observation could be made concerning the evaluation of eucharistic practice. For instance, it is possible to focus on particular aspects of representation: a theological evaluation of the Eucharist might focus on the significance of certain ritual movements and actions utilized by a priest at the altar, and miss the fact that most people in the congregation have never noticed these actions for the simple reason that they usually have their eyes closed at this point in the service![319]

Theology and Performance

The Eucharist offers a case study of the way that, in the expression and the life of the Christian community, the performance of 'theology' operates at a number of levels. The interpretation of the Eucharist based on production, representation and audience shows how biblical and theological texts form part of the lived-in tradition of the community. In performance they are taken up in particular representations and find a place in the lived experience of individuals and communities. This

---

318 The same cannot be said for a band like Led Zeppelin, where Jimmy Page was deeply influenced by the occultist Alistair Crowley.

319 That is, unless they come from St Stephen's House of course, which is probably the reason why they stand during the Eucharist so they can see the actions of the celebrating clergy person.

form of analysis is not locked into the oppositional dualism associated with modern theology. Through this analytical framework experience and doctrine are seen as interrelating rather than as alternatives that must be reduced to the other. At the same time the theological in terms of the doctrinal and the historical is also not reduced to the cultural. Rather it is seen as part of a living tradition that is moving and changing as it is represented and as it is used in the shaping of communal and individual identity. The critical and creative functions of the theologian, be they doctrinal, systematic or liturgical, are seen as a vital part of the way that the tradition is generated and renews itself. At the same time the processes of production are seen as part of expression and communal life.

Performance relates to the way that texts are animated in their use. There is an ongoing dynamic which operates at the level of representation. In performance inscribed meanings associated with production shift and form new connections through articulation. What is true for the Eucharist is also true for 'theology' more generally. The productive process results in the formation of texts. These representations, in an academic context, may be lectures or academic books. Representation, however, also relates to all the ways that individuals and communities express faith, in lifestyles, prayers, and other means. Expression also includes material culture such as gravestones, church buildings, adverts in magazines, and so on. In performance, theology is seen as part of a moving ecosystem. In the Eucharist theology is animated and set in motion as a lived-in culture. It is therefore an embodied 'theology'. This cultural reading of the theological, however, also implies that it is simultaneously a place of spiritual significance and experience. The performance of the Eucharist mediates divine encounter. This mediation is not an interpretive layer placed over the cultural. The indwelt-ness of the Eucharist is there in the biblical text of the words of institution. It is there in the way that this text has been 'produced' through liturgical and theological scholarship. It is there in representation and it is there in the way that individuals and communities make meaning and identity in relation to performance. In performance the discursive practices of the Christian community are seen as being a place of divine participation. In performance individuals and communities are 'indwelt'. There is then a relationship between the way that representation and discourses are animated in the Christian community and the mediation of the life of God. This is true for the communion service but is also true for theological expression more generally.

Part 3

Liquid Church and a Consuming Faith

8

Things

Liquid Church expresses the way that ecclesial being is extended and made fluid through mediation. The liquid Church moves beyond the traditional boundaries of congregation and denomination through the use of communication and information technologies. These mediations circulate and set in motion theological expression. Participation and communion are then mediated in the lifestyles and identities that communities and individuals construct as they participate in this flow of representation. Participation in the mediated religious culture of the liquid Church is thus a consuming faith. Consuming because it is contextualized in the ways of operating associated with popular culture, but it is consuming 'faith' because it is participation and attention. Consuming is therefore animation and participation as it mediates the Trinitarian life of God.

In the liquid Church to participate in the circulation of the flow of theological representation is to be attentive. Consuming faith is not inevitably or necessarily a place of communion. From the discussion of mission studies it is clear that the translation of faith in a cultural context is problematic. The Church adopts culture in order to communicate and connect, but as it does so it must also seek to adapt and transform the culture in which it is situated. This process is far from straightforward. Culture is messy and there is no unambiguous and uncontaminated place from which to view culture because it is not only the water in which we all swim, it is also the substance from which all ecclesial life is constructed. By adopting ways of seeing drawn from cultural studies, practical theology can interact with the liquid nature of the contemporary Church. It is a missiological necessity to find ways to critique and correct mediation and expression, and yet this is a practical theology that operates within and through the flow. It is, as I have already pointed out, a practical theology without guarantees. It is the realization that liquid Church is only Church as it mediates Christ that must remain the focus of this form of practical theology. At the same time, because it is through participation in the circulation of representation that this joining to Christ in the body of the Church is made incarnate, practical theology must engage with the material culture of things.

Material Christianity

During the 1990s the WWJD teen craze swept through the Christian world. WWJD was an abbreviated form of the phrase 'What Would Jesus Do?' WWJD was woven into small colourful bracelets that could be worn around the wrist or the ankle. The original bracelets were intended to be worn by young people as a way of reminding them that they were called to live their lives as disciples of Christ. At the end of the decade the US-based magazine *Group* reported that Christian retailers had sold 15 million WWJD bracelets worldwide.[320] As well as bracelets WWJD was marketed as an album of music, a board game and as a variety of fashion items. Bo Cassell observed that the WWJD phenomenon had grown to such an extent that, 'the bracelets created a grass-roots buzz that eventually fueled a product-selling frenzy. You can get almost anything with WWJD on it – jewelry, T-shirts, posters, coins, key chains – almost everything but cigarettes and soft drinks.'[321]

Popular culture is produced and reproduced through the manufacture and circulation of things. Products are commodified and marketed by the culture industry. They are in turn bought and used by people as a part of identity formation. Style is made up of the arrangement of things and the meanings that these things carry as they are variously associated and displayed. The WWJD phenomenon is a contemporary illustration of the way that young Christians have sought to contextualize their expression of faith by adopting the form of popular culture. The WWJD bracelet is just the latest example of what Colleen McDannell calls 'material Christianity'.[322]

---

320 Cassell, B. (1999), 'WWJD', *Group Magazine*, March/April.
321 Cassell, 'WWJD'.
322 McDannell, C. (1995), *Material Christianity: Religion and Popular Culture in America*, New Haven: Yale University Press.

In *Material Christianity* McDannell analyses the significance of artefacts and landscapes for the development of religious identity in America. Alongside the various products associated with the Jesus Movement and evangelical retailing since the 1960s she also discusses the symbolism of the Laurel Hill cemetery, the significance of the Bible in the Victorian home and the circulation of water from the shrine at Lourdes among the Catholic community. There has been a tendency in the study of religion, says McDannell, to pass over or treat as superficial the way that religious communities make use of objects and landscapes. She argues that American Christian identity is closely related to material culture and that, '"genuine" religion has always been expressed and made real with objects, architecture, art, and landscapes'.[323]

Objects are particularly important in the lives of ordinary Christians. Artefacts enable believers to exchange gifts, to maintain relationships with family and with the characters in their supernatural world. Material goods are a means to create and arrange their religious world. The use of things in religious life tells Christians that they are part of a community, and that they belong.[324] McDannell argues that, 'While some Christians accomplish the same thing through the exchange of ideas, many prefer to interact with visual and sensual symbols. Religious meaning is not merely inherited or simply accessed through the intellect. Orthodox statements of belief and formal rituals are only one part of the complicated structure of religion.'[325] So for McDannell things relate to practices and identity. She does not deny the significance of 'ideas' circulating and reinforcing identity. Rather she points out that for many people things are preferred. This is very similar to David Morgan's discussion of the visual in relation to religious art.

Morgan's study of the practices associated with the religious images of the artist Warner Sallman draws on McDannell's work on material culture. Morgan describes what he calls 'visual piety'. Visual piety is seen in the way that images are linked to particular sacred ideas, to ways of looking, and to the practices of everyday life.[326] 'Looking at

323 McDannell, *Material*, p. 272.
324 McDannell, *Material*, p. 272.
325 McDannell, *Material*, p. 272.
326 Morgan, D. (1998), *Visual Piety: A History and Theory of Popular Religious Images*, Berkeley: University of California Press, pp. 3ff.

images, giving and receiving them, conducting prayer and Bible study before them, displaying them in the home, handing them on to the next generation – these are some of the iconic practices of belief, acts of visual piety.'[327] Morgan and McDannell's work on the extent that lived religion is associated with things is in many ways parallel to the way that cultural studies interprets commodities in relation to the meanings made by those who consume them.

Meaning and Things

Paul du Gay and his co-authors argue that things should be read in association with the meanings that they carry, and in turn these meanings are seen as part of a system of meanings.[328] As we have seen, the authors illustrate this understanding of things and meaning through an analysis of the Sony Walkman as a cultural artefact. The Walkman, they argue, has associated meanings that we are able to read and interpret. It is cultural because of these meanings. So, 'the Walkman is cultural because we have constituted it as a meaningful object. We can talk, think about and imagine it.'[329] It is cultural because it is associated with particular practices and places, such as listening to music on trains, or while walking in the street, or when exercising. It is cultural because it is associated with particular kinds of people, such as young people, students, and tourists walking round art galleries. The Walkman, they suggest, has a 'social profile or identity'.[330] It has a place in our culture because it is frequently represented in the media and in advertising and movies. 'The image of the Sony Walkman – sleek high-tech, functional in design, miniaturized – has become a sort of metaphor which stands for or represents a distinctively late-modern, technological culture or way of life.'[331] It is therefore possible to study the Walkman as a way to access the practices and meanings within contemporary culture and society.

---

327 Morgan, *Visual*, p. 4.
328 Du Gay, P., Hall, S., Janes, L., Mackay, H. and Negus, K. (1997), *Doing Cultural Studies: The Story of the Sony Walkman*, London: Sage.
329 Du Gay, *Doing*, p. 10.
330 Du Gay, *Doing*, p. 10.
331 Du Gay, *Doing*, p. 11.

The Walkman has been replaced by digital technology, yet it remains the case that this kind of electronic 'thing' has a cultural significance. The significance of the thing comes from its ability to carry meaning. Meaning comes from the way it is represented in advertising and the media, from the practices of those that use it and the way that these practices form part of identity or a way of life, and from our capability of reading the Walkman as a meaningful object. What holds true for the Walkman in this sense is also true for the iPod, the MP3 player and indeed for the mobile phone.

Style and the Meaning of Things

Things are used as part of lived and meaningful practice as they are connected with other things in a style. In cultural studies style has been understood as the way that subcultural groups construct identity and belonging around the arrangement of things.[332] Stuart Hall argued that subcultures create a new unity of meanings, or a style, by the combination of a variety of what he calls symbolic 'bits':

> The new meanings emerge because the 'bits' which had been borrowed or revived are brought together into a new and distinctive stylistic ensemble: but also because symbolic objects – dress – appearance, language, ritual occasions, styles of interaction were made to form a unity ...'[333]

For Hall the significance of subcultural style was to be found in the way that young people arranged the various bits into a meaningful whole. This whole could be read as a form of resistance and protest.

This interpretation of style as meaningful resistant statement has been most closely associated with Dick Hebdige's *Subculture: The Meaning of Style*.[334] Hebdige argues that there is a need to go below the surface of particular subcultural styles to understand their meaning.

---

332 Subculture has been variously understood in cultural studies and sociology more generally. For an account of the developments in subcultural theory, see Gelder, K. and Thornton, S. (eds) (1997), *The Subcultures Reader*, London: Routledge.

333 Hall, S. and Jefferson, T. (eds) (1975), *Resistance Through Rituals: Youth Subcultures in Post-war Britain*, London: Hutchinson, p. 56.

334 Hebdige, D. (1979), *Subculture: The Meaning of Style*, London: Methuen.

The ideological meaning of signs needs to be 'uncovered' by disentangling the various codes within which they are organized.[335] The struggle, which exists between different discourses within ideology, according to Hebdige, is played out within signification. There is conflict around the possession and interpretation of the sign.[336] Youth cultures participate in these struggles by the appropriation of particular fashion items, which then act as signs.

> safety pins and Vaseline ... are open to double inflection: to illegitimate as well as legitimate uses. These humble objects can be magically appropriated; 'stolen' by subordinate groups and made to carry 'secret' meaning: meanings which express, in code a form of resistance to the order which guarantees their continued subordination.[337]

Hebdige describes this creative process by drawing on the concept of 'bricolage', by which he means the appropriation and juxtaposition of a variety of symbolic elements. New styles often arise as two incompatible elements are brought together, for example, 'flag: jacket', 'hole: T-shirt', 'comb: weapon'.[338] Hebdige uses the term 'homology' to describe the unity that comes about by the process of combining elements into a style. He argues that spectacular subcultures can be read as resistance, but they are also a significant challenge to the symbolic order of mainstream society. In describing this he adopts Umberto Eco's phrase 'semiotic guerrilla warfare'.[339] Subcultural style is therefore a kind of underground battle raged at the level of the sign. A distinctive aspect of the argument in *Subculture: The Meaning of Style* is Hebdige's assertion that white youth subcultures in Britain are developed in relation to black subcultures, and, in particular, black popular music. Thus subcultural style is seen as a series of 'deep-structural adaptations which symbolically accommodate or expunge the black presence from the host community'.[340] Hebdige argues that subcultural style can be read in this manner only at its point of origin. As the style becomes more widely adopted and taken up by the fashion industry

---

335 Hebdige, *Subculture*, p. 13.
336 Hebdige, *Subculture*, p. 17.
337 Hebdige, *Subculture*, p. 18.
338 Hebdige, *Subculture*, p. 106.
339 Hebdige, *Subculture*, p. 105.
340 Hebdige, *Subculture*, p. 44.

its meaning becomes diluted. This process is unavoidable. 'Youth cultural styles may begin by issuing symbolic challenges, but they must inevitably end by establishing new sets of conventions; by creating new commodities, new industries, rejuvenating old ones ...'[341]

Material Culture and the Jesus Movement

The WWJD bracelet is part of the material culture of evangelicalism. It does not necessarily carry the shock value of the safety pin or the bondage trouser, but it forms part of the subcultural identity of the movement. WWJD illustrates the way that evangelical Christians have adopted forms of expression that are common in popular culture. The bracelet is one small part of a much larger Christian subculture with its own music, T-shirts, celebrities, festivals, magazines, and so on. This subculture has its origins in the Jesus Movement that started in the USA during the 1970s. *Selling Worship*[342] argues that the Jesus Movement had a decisive impact on the culture of contemporary Church both in the UK and in the USA. The Jesus Movement came about as young people who had been caught up in the hippie movement of the late 1960s started to turn towards the Christian religion. 'In the atmosphere of disappointment and depression that followed the conflicts and failures of the sixties, many youths sought out alternative religious movements.'[343] Some of these young people were disorientated by drugs, says Tipton, and they found work life to be a disappointment and so as they grew older they found that religion offered them a way to come to terms with American society.[344] On the west coast and around the USA, churches such as Calvary Chapel in Santa Ana California and its minister, Chuck Smith, began to orientate their work around these disillusioned hippies.[345]

As these young people 'turned on to Jesus' they became known as

341 Hebdige, *Subculture*, p. 86.
342 Ward, P. (2005), *Selling Worship*, Carlisle: Paternoster.
343 Tipton, S. M. (1982), *Getting Saved From the Sixties*, Berkeley: University of California Press, p. 30.
344 Tipton, *Getting*, p. 30.
345 Miller, D. E. (1997), *Reinventing American Protestantism: Christianity in the New Millennium*, Berkeley: University of California Press, pp. 27ff.

Jesus freaks or Jesus people.[346] They attracted attention because while they seemed to be adopting conservative and Pentecostal forms of Christianity, at the same time they kept their hippie style. The result was that these young people transformed the normally reserved and culturally conservative expression of US Churches. Writing at the time, sociologists Enroth, Ericson and Peters observed that churches such as Calvary Chapel had become a 'new kind of undenominational "hip" church'.[347] Being a 'hip' Christian involved participation in a new form of youth-orientated religious subculture.

The Jesus Movement birthed an explosion in subcultural consumer products. This was the material culture of the Jesus revolution. Products linked to the movement included Jesus revolution bumper stickers, fish pendants, 'Smile Jesus loves you' stickers and a range of T-shirts, psychedelic Bible covers and bookmarks.[348] McDannell points out that the Jesus Movement led to a revival in the fortunes of Christian retailing. Between 1965 and 1975 the number of independent Christian bookstores in the USA more than doubled from 725 stores to 1,850.[349] In publishing also the Jesus revolution produced its own best sellers. *The Late Great Planet Earth*,[350] written by the Jesus Movement leader Hal Lindsey in 1970, examined current events and found in them an indication that we were living in the end times. Lindsey hit a nerve because apocalyptic speculation was a major interest among the Jesus people. Published by Zondervan in 1970 the book had sold 9 million copies by 1978.[351] The impact of the new youth style also extended to the publication of Bibles. In 1971 *The Living Bible*, a modern-day transliteration of the biblical text, was published. By the end of the year it had sold one million copies and by 1975 over 18 million had been sold. McDannell argues that *The Living Bible* served to 'sacralize' the contemporary language of these young Christians.[352] In *The Living Bible* hip and contemporary language replaced traditional biblical

---

346 Enroth, R. M., Ericson, E. E. and Peters, C. B. (1972), *The Story of the Jesus People: A Factual Survey*, Exeter: Paternoster Press, p. 9.
347 Enroth, *Story*, p. 85.
348 McDannell, *Material*, pp. 246ff.
349 McDannell, *Material*, p. 246.
350 Lindsey, H. (1970), *The Late Great Planet Earth*, Grand Rapids: Zondervan.
351 McDannell, *Material*, p. 248.
352 McDannell, *Material*, p. 248.

phrases. So in the US edition we read that the Lord is a 'flashlight' to our feet and Moses goes to the 'bathroom'.

There has always been a close association between the development of youth subcultures and popular music. The Jesus Movement was no exception to this rule. During the 1970s there was an explosion in what was known as Jesus rock music. Artists such as Larry Norman burst onto the Christian scene. In the UK musicians such as the young Graham Kendrick and the folk group Parchment along with musicals such as *Godspell* and later *Come Together* brought the style and expression of the US youth-oriented evangelical Christianity to the notice of the churches. *Come Together* was significant because it made the connection between charismatic worship and the Jesus Movement and it could be argued that this musical on its own led to the birth of the contemporary charismatic worship scene in the UK.

A Mediated Religious Culture

The Jesus Movement transformed evangelical Christianity, reconstituting it as a kind of youth-oriented subculture. The subculture was produced and mediated through the action of a range of media-based activities, and these included record companies, magazine publishing, and new kinds of youth-based festivals, as well as the production of Bibles and popular religious books. For young people suddenly there was a Christian youth style. Christian identity increasingly revolved around the production and consumption of these products. The mediated religious culture extended to the expression of the Church through the contemporary worship songs and styles of charismatic celebration. The new style of expression could be experienced by an increasing number of people in the UK through the newly established festivals and events such as Greenbelt, Spring Harvest, and New Wine/Soul Survivor. These events have become sites for the marketing and exchange of new expressions of the faith. Church members and leaders attend these events, they sing the new songs and listen to the new ideas, buy the books, the magazines, and of course the T-shirt, and they take them back to their communities. Through these forms of mediation the evangelical subculture is extended to the local church.[353]

---

353 For more on this see Ward, *Selling*.

The contemporary mediated religious culture has grown directly from the link made by the Jesus Movement between the forms of expression and style in youth culture and evangelical faith. This articulation has created a momentum associated with the logic of the Christian culture industry. As in the wider popular culture in the Christian world there is a particular pace of change, which is associated with the production and circulation of representation. This pace means that evangelical culture is generated as a constantly changing cycle of representation. New songs, new personalities, new forms of worship are generated and circulated through the action of the media. The annual cycle of events and festivals means that each year there is a new songbook, a new theme to be explored and a new initiative for mission and evangelism. Christian organizations and publishing companies have increasingly geared themselves around these events.

Practical Theology and Subcultural Style

The WWJD bracelet is an indication of the extent to which evangelical identity has been formed around mediation. This small fashion item is significant because it shows how the evangelical subculture has been able to adopt the language of youth culture. The bracelet operates as a cultural object in that it is situated in the signifying system of style. It may not carry the shock associated with say punk or goth style, but for the average Christian young person it can be seen to function as a resistant symbol.

The WWJD bracelet has a good deal in common with the 'silver ring'. In 2007 a Christian teenager, Lynda Playfoot, took her school to the high court in Britain arguing that the school breached her human rights by not allowing her to wear her silver ring.[354] 'The silver ring thing' is a movement that was first launched in the United States in 1996 by evangelical Christians. The movement was started with the intention of encouraging young people to abstain from sexual activity before marriage. As a sign of commitment to sexual purity young people were encouraged to purchase and wear the silver ring. The court case in the UK, despite the reservation that comes from the fact that Lynda Playfoot's

---

354 Reported in *The Times*, 22 June 2007.

parents were involved in promoting the silver ring organization, is an indication of the extent to which the products of the evangelical sub-culture carry meaning. For young Christians the material symbols of their faith that are generated by the mediated religious culture of the evangelical scene have increasingly become a focus for identity and be-longing. With the silver ring and the WWJD bracelet there is a connec-tion between theological and moral teaching and a particular product. The ideas are mediated through the representation associated with a material object. The meaning of the object lies in a complex interplay between the interests and actions of Christian organizations, religious communities and the practices of young people in adopting the style.

These relations are repeated in the evangelical discourse, not just in youth crazes but perhaps more significantly through the changes in styles of worship and ways of being church. For practical theology to engage fully with what it means to be Christian in this mediated religious culture there is a need to examine the link between represen-tation, processes of production and the ways that products shape the lived experience of communities and individuals. The way of seeing drawn from cultural studies focuses attention on the way that identity is situated in the interplay of these relations. This means for instance that it is not sufficient simply to examine the way that commercial companies operate as powerful culture industries within the Chris-tian subculture and critique these as a form of manipulation. The next chapter examines this culture industry critique in more depth, but for the moment it is sufficient to make the point that this kind of analysis needs to be balanced with the way that social relations through the construction of identities mediate meaning in relation to these kinds of products. This means that practical theology must find ways to under-stand and evaluate how young Christians make use of things as they seek to express their faith as a form of difference and resistance in their local communities and schools. At the same time there are problems with the development of a mediated religious culture.

Contradictions in the Liquid Church

Through the processes of production and representation a mediated religious culture circulates theology in a material culture. These actions animate and extend ecclesial being, making it more fluid and liquid. This liquid Church circulates within and beyond the traditional boundaries of the congregation and denominational structures. Participation in this circulation operates as a form of attention, but as it does so it generates an ambiguous ecclesial space, which carries its own contradictions.

Popular culture is generated in and through group identity in relation to mediation, but this identity is a 'subculture', that is, it is a difference in relation to other subcultures. As contemporary evangelical Christianity has developed, it has increasingly mirrored youth culture in developing its products and style. Starting in the 1970s mainly among young people, this evangelical subcultural style has colonized the adult Church and through festivals such as Spring Harvest and Greenbelt it has had an impact way beyond the evangelical constituency. At the same time the success of this style has brought tensions and problems because as it has generated a sense of belonging, it has also brought separation. This means that as Christian young people, and the Christian community, have adopted this style they have simultaneously been defining themselves within the wider culture by difference. So as the material culture of the mediated liquid Church has been a source of identification it has simultaneously acted to reinforce a tendency towards a sense of identity and distinction within popular culture for many Christians. This movement towards difference I would suggest underlies some of the conflict between evangelicals and other traditions in the Church. Yet tensions within denominations may not be the most significant effect of mediation. There are important missiological issues here. The strengthening of Christian identity in relation to circulation of expression can serve to distract attention from the ebb and flow of spirituality in popular culture more generally. The strong link between specifically Christian forms of representation and subcultural style as distinction and difference can operate as a disincentive to further efforts towards contextualization. This has a direct impact on the way that ministry operates in relation to young people, for instance. A strong emphasis on the development of a distinctive Christian subcultural style will mean that mission is orientated around attracting young people into the Christian cultural group. Where the identification between faith and mediated culture become absolutized any attempt to contextualize faith among non-Christian young people is seen as syncretistic. The irony and contradiction here is that this critique of relational forms of contextual ministry ignores the moves that were made in the 1970s towards the expression of faith in popular culture. This kind of observation should serve to introduce a note of caution in practical theology as it attempts to offer a critical evaluation of mediated religious culture. There are both positives and negatives in the way that mediation has brought about changes in the contemporary Church. Liquid Church, in its fluid animation of meaning in relation to things, muddies the water.

9

The Christian Culture Industry

In *Consuming Religion* Vincent Miller argues that a consumer culture represents a significant challenge for the Christian faith.[355] Consumer culture, he says, commodifies religious symbols and practices. This is corrosive because commodification unhooks practices and symbols from historic traditions and communities of faith.[356] As a committed Catholic Miller is concerned that religious cultures and communities should attempt to resist the negative effects of consumerism. Yet he is also highly critical of theological engagement with consumer culture. Theologians, he says, prefer to discuss consumerism in relation to the history of ideas and anthropology. For Miller this is a mistake. 'Whatever the origins of consumer desire in modern metaphysics and anthropology, it is currently sustained not primarily by an incorrigible commitment to pernicious ideas but by a host of economic, social and cultural structures and practices.'[357] Central to these processes are the mediating actions of the culture industry. As the contemporary Church has embraced forms of communication drawn from popular culture it has generated its own Christian culture industry.

Miller is critical of the impact of consumer culture on the Church and in the wider culture. My own view is that this is unhelpfully pessimistic. Through mediation the expression of the Church is extended and becomes more fluid. As it circulates it is animated and set in motion and in the freedom of the Spirit it may become participation in the divine life. At the same time there are tensions and contradictions in this contextualization of faith in a mediated religious culture. Consumer culture is not necessarily corrosive, it is simply a muddied flow of the

---

355 Miller, V. J. (2004), *Consuming Religion*, London: Continuum, p. 72.
356 Miller, *Consuming*, p. 13.
357 Miller, *Consuming*, p. 115.

helpful and the unhelpful. It is a place where epiphany and attention coexist with a veiling and concealing of the divine light. As we have seen, this muddied arena of mediation is evident in the material culture of contemporary Christianity but it is no less true when it comes to the productive action of the Christian culture industries. This means that practical theology must negotiate a complex area when it comes to a critical evaluation of the way that the processes of production shape the liquid Church. A reflex judgement that the culture industries are necessarily a dumbing down of faith, or that they are in the thrall of capitalist economics, will only serve to obscure the way that production sets 'theology' in motion and facilitates animation. At the same time an uncritical acceptance of the Christian culture industry is also problematic because it is in danger of ignoring the way that production has a logic that can lead towards the distortion of faith. These kinds of judgements are made even more complex because they operate in a field of play that is orientated around questions of taste in relation to theological expression. The link between taste and the evaluation of the Christian culture industry is inherently complex because it articulates social class with ecclesial identities and distinctions.

Culture Industry and the Contemporary Church

As contemporary Christians contextualize faith in popular culture they are adopting processes of production that are akin to the wider cultural industries. This move towards a Christian cultural industry is most highly developed in the area of worship music. Two contemporary Churches illustrate the way that ecclesial life is shifting and becoming more fluid through these cultural practices. These Churches are Vineyard and Hillsong. Vineyard has its origins in the the 1970s and 1980s and the charismatic ministry of John Wimber. From a single church in California it has now spread to more than 1,500 churches worldwide.[358] Hillsong has similarly grown from the Pentecostal ministry of Brian and Bobbie Houston in Sydney, Australia, where its congregation currently attracts around 20,000 people. This mega-church has planted sizeable congregations in London, Kiev and Paris.[359] Although

---

358 www.vineyardusa.org/about/history.aspx accessed 5 Feb. 2008.
359 www2.hillsong.com/church/default.asp?pid'10 accessed 5 Feb. 2008.

they are in many ways very different, what Hillsong and Vineyard have in common is an emphasis upon worship music, and both have established recording companies as a part of their church's ministry.

The Vineyard music website greets the visitor with the following message: 'Welcome. In fulfilling our mission to encourage all people to pursue a deeper relationship with God, the Vineyard Movement has offices around the world dedicated to worship through songs, music, resources and events. Please choose the office closest to where you live to find out more. Thanks for passing through.'[360] The web page then offers a series of links to Vineyard music websites in different parts of the world. As well as the USA and the UK these include links to record distribution companies, music publishers and record companies based in Brazil, Canada, Germany and Austria, Scandinavia and South Africa. For the Vineyard churches, record companies are part of their ministry and mission. Vineyard Records UK describe their purpose in terms of a 'worship ministry' that serves the wider Church with 'resources, training and music that enables today's church to worship God in a manner that is culture-current'.[361]

Hillsong describe the aims of their record company, Hillsong Music, in very similar terms to the Vineyard churches. In 2006 the Hillsong Music website explained their activities with a corporate mission statement:

Who is Hillsong Music Australia: The resource arm of Hillsong Church. Hillsong Music Australia was birthed from the vision God gave for Hillsong Church. Hillsong Music plays an integral part in that overall vision and its growth over the past few years reveals God's blessing and provision for Hillsong Church in so many ways. Our Purpose: Hillsong Music is a vital component in the ministry that God has entrusted to Hillsong Church, its primary function being to resource the church world-wide. To enable people to enter into an atmosphere of worshipping the Lord by providing resources that help churches break into another dimension of worship. To empower people, ministries and churches through teaching, leadership and of course, praise and worship. To take the blessing and anoint-

360 www.vmg.com/ accessed 5 Feb. 08.
361 www.vineyardrecords.co.uk/ministry/index.html accessed 5 Feb. 2008.

ing God has placed on Hillsong Church beyond our walls to the nation of Australia and the nations of the world. It is a privilege to be able to equip and serve in this way. Our prayer is that you will succeed in every endeavour you are called to pursue.[362]

Vineyard and Hillsong are examples of the way that the contemporary Church has created a Christian culture industry. Through the action of record companies and the associated websites and other means of distribution, their own distinctive style of worship music is produced, promoted and sold around the world. A key phrase that both Hillsong and Vineyard have in common is the word 'resource'. Resource basically means product or commodity that is being offered for sale. Clicking on 'Resources' on any of the websites takes you to an online store that is full of worship-related products. 'Resource' articulates with help, encouragement and the animation of worshipping communities beyond their own specific church. These products are therefore presented as services to help the wider Church to engage with a charismatic form of worship and experience. Through the means of commodification a specific form of spirituality is therefore transmitted, set in motion and circulated. Hillsong and Vineyard see this as their mission and gift to the worldwide Church. So by embracing the productive processes of the Christian cultural industry they are able to have an impact beyond their own individual congregations.

Through the circulation of songs, mediated in recordings, DVDs, downloads and songbooks, evangelical Christians are able to participate in the animation of a distinctive spiritual practice of worship. The Christian culture industry therefore creates through these mediating actions a consumer-based spirituality. This spirituality is contextualized within the cultural logic of popular culture to the extent that it is orientated towards a continual production of new forms of representation. The charismatic Christian culture industry is based around a cycle that produces a flow of new songs, new recordings, new bands and worship leaders. This drive towards a circulation of new products leads to the generation of an ever-changing pattern of worship festivals, concert tours, and worship leader training events. These activities

---

362 Source http://secure.hillsong.com accessed 29 Sept. 2006.

shape the way that the contemporary Church becomes more fluid in a flow of representation beyond the traditional forms of congregational life.

The Christian culture industries extend the local expression of the Church through mediation, but they do not replace the local Christian community. The mediated nature of the contemporary worship scene is produced within the context of local worshipping communities. The worship leaders have an authenticity because they participate in the life of these local (albeit often extraordinary) congregations. The songs therefore arise from a context but they are in turn consumed in a locality. Through consumption the songs are mediated within a local context as worship bands in churches around the world use them and make them their own. There is also a trans-local or globalizing dynamic in the mediating action of the Christian culture industries. The circulation of expression through mediation means that there is a charismatic style that exists at the level of representation in the inscribed texts of the movement. In this circulating dynamic beyond the local congregation, texts have a relationship with each other and form articulations through connection. This may be as simple as the way that Hillsong and Vineyard songs might be included on the same worship CD or songbook collection, but it may also operate in the way that the charismatic culture evolves and develops. For example, different songs and worship artists may be influenced by particular forms of lyrical or musical expression as they participate in and consume the products (or resources) that are circulating through mediation.

Practical Theology and the High Culture/Low Culture Debate

The Christian culture industry has developed from the contextualizing impulse of the contemporary Church, but contextualization, because it is a negotiation of faith within culture, is never straightforward. In fact it is often muddied, confusing and conflicted. Practical theology is a discipline of discernment where the Church critically reflects on its own expression. This means that it is crucial to find appropriate frameworks for understanding the Christian culture industry as an aspect of popular culture. This discussion of the culture industry is set within the long-held view that culture can be divided between its high forms and its low forms. This view, first associated with Matthew Arnold, has exercised an enduring influence on theological approaches to all aspects of popular culture.

Arnold, writing in the 1860s, sets culture in opposition to what he calls 'anarchy'. Culture, says Arnold, relates to the way that 'great men of culture' have had a passion to propagate the 'best knowledge, the best ideas of their time'. These men have worked, says Arnold, to over-come what is 'harsh, uncouth, difficult, abstract and professional', to spread 'sweetness and light' beyond the 'clique of the cultivated and learned'.[363] Anarchy is the modern spirit to 'do what one likes'. It is linked to a 'blind faith' in machinery without regard for what that machinery is created for. [364] So Arnold sets up a relationship of opposi-tion based around modern mechanical culture presented as anarchy, and his idea of culture as the best ideas and knowledge championed by the educated. For Storey this use of anarchy in Arnold's work 'operates as a synonym for popular culture'.[365] It is the responsibility of educa-tion and the educated to overcome anarchy through the processes of education that should be open to all. So the high culture/low culture divide is framed around an elitist view of culture and an egalitarian ideal of education that reaches beyond the elite.

The culture and anarchy thesis has had a deep and continuing influ-ence on the debate concerning the shape of the contemporary Church. An example of this is Richard Holloway's fabulously bitchy complaint that evangelicals appear to be too ready to embrace bad taste in order that they might be able to spread the gospel. Clearly such a thing is really unthinkable as far as Holloway is concerned. He contrasts what he sees as a mainstream or developed Christian aesthetic in worship, art and architecture with the popularizing evangelical tendency, which he characterizes as, 'a sort of aesthetic contraction and banality in which liturgy is fast food rather than haute cuisine'.[366] Holloway's comments

---

363 Arnold, M. (1869), *Culture and Anarchy* (1932 edn), Cambridge: Cambridge University Press, p. 70.

364 Arnold, *Anarchy*, p. 76.

365 Storey, J. (ed.) (1994), *Cultural Theory and Popular Culture: A Reader*, Hemel Hempstead: Harvester Wheatsheaf, p. 3.

366 Holloway, R. (1993), 'An Outsider's Perspective', in France, R. T. and McGrath, A. E. (eds), *Evangelical Anglicans: Their Influence in the Church Today*, London: SPCK, pp. 181–2.

show how judgements about theology and the Church get tangled up in issues of taste. Taste is problematic because judgements concerning what is 'best', especially when it comes to areas such as music or art or literature, tend to reveal as much about the person making the judgement as they do about the work of art itself. So judgements about the expression of the Church are vulnerable to a similar sort of criticism to that which has been made of the culture and anarchy thesis as a whole, namely that what is 'best' seems to depend on who is making the decision.

Holloway's treatment of evangelicalism opens up another area of the high culture/low culture debate. It is not just that evangelical culture is fast-food religion rather than haute cuisine, and therefore an affront to good taste; perhaps more importantly the willingness of evangelicals to embrace popular forms of expression represents a rejection of the improving and educational calling of a religious high culture. To embrace the popular is to shift the Church from the ranks of the cultured and culturing to those of anarchy and low culture. As has already been discussed, Raymond Williams suggests that the idea of culture emerges from cultivation as an agricultural process.[367] To be cultured was to have been grown correctly or been nurtured in the right way. So culture has strong links to whatever we feel is of value or of worth. These are the things that society wishes to pass on to the next generation. When this rather emotive content is mixed with a sensibility that identifies particular forms of theological expression as mediators of value then we can see some of the energy that lies behind our ecclesiastical 'culture wars'.

As any youth worker will tell you, the Church seems to be able to generate quite heated conflicts around these issues. I remember being hauled over the coals quite early in my youth work career by an irate vicar who felt that I was corrupting the youth group through popular culture. What sparked this tirade was a meeting where I invited the young people to bring along some music they liked. The idea was we played it and then we talked about what it meant to them. It all went quite well until one of the young people played their favourite song, Marc Almond singing *Tainted Love*. The vicar was in the next room

367 See Williams, R. (1976), *Keywords: A Vocabulary of Culture and Society*, Glasgow: Fontana.

arranging chairs and he didn't like what he heard. I was told the next day that it was not my job to promote pop culture and I was to focus on encouraging only a Christian approach to issues like love.

For practical theology a critique of the Christian culture industry based on the high culture/low culture understanding is problematic. Theological judgements become clouded as they are mixed with cultural taste and yet there always remains the question of what is of worth and of enduring value. These issues continue to exercise a powerful gravitational pull not only in theological discussion but also in popular culture itself.[368] A good example of this is seen in the popularity of television programmes based on the format of 'the hundred best'. The hundred best can be based on, films, musicals, TV soaps or pop songs. Whatever the subject, the format is very simple: 'the audience' has voted for the best whatever, and as a result they have been placed in an order. Much of the pleasure in this kind of programme is derived from our tendency to disagree or agree about the relative worth of a song, a film, or whatever. Behind these sorts of disputes it is clear that popular culture is never devoid of issues related to value or worth; it has just repositioned who decides on these questions. So what is high and what is low is reframed by popular culture while still leaving in play questions related to judgement and taste.

Mass Culture and the Culture Industry

The high/low view of culture has been closely linked to the critique of the culture industry. The idea of the culture industry has its origins in the work of Theodor Adorno and those associated with the Frankfurt school of social research.[369] Adorno and others within the Frankfurt school fled Nazi Germany for the United States in the 1930s. It was this group which first coined the phrase 'mass culture' to describe Nazi propaganda, and then later it was applied to the popular culture of

---

368 For an example of a theological approach to the high culture/low culture debate, see Gorringe, T. (2004), *Furthering Humanity: A Theology of Culture*, Aldershot: Ashgate. Gorringe, however, is critical of a media-based popular culture and echoes Hoggart's advocacy of a popular folk culture. He makes the link between folk culture and liberation theology as the basis for a theological approach to cultural practice.

369 McGuigan, J. (1992), *Cultural Populism*, London: Routledge, p. 47.

the United States. Adorno explains, however, that in his work with Horkheimer the term 'culture industry' was introduced in preference to 'mass culture'.[370] He abandoned the term 'mass culture' because it was seen as carrying the possibility of an interpretation of culture as that which arises from the people, that is, from below, whereas Adorno was at pains to describe the process whereby the 'culture industry' imposes itself from above: 'The customer is not king, as the culture industry would have us believe, not its subject, but its object.'[371]

Adorno argued that popular culture, and in particular the popular song, was crucially shaped by industrial processes. The term industrial does not refer to the way that cultural items are manufactured. Rather he is drawing attention to what he calls 'standardization' and the rationalization of distribution.[372] Standardization produces patterned and unimaginative cultural products. These are produced to satisfy the lowest common denominator in the consumer. Workers on the factory line or in offices demand entertainment, they seek novelty, but they do so, argues Adorno, with an inability to make any effort. Workers seek 'effortless sensation'.[373] The result is a standardized and undemanding repetition of familiar and reassuring patterns in films, music, and so forth. It is the culture industry that feeds, and in part produces, this cycle of boredom, entertainment and return to boredom.

By drawing attention to the industrial elements in contemporary popular culture Adorno made a major contribution to cultural studies. The circumstances under which cultural texts are produced and marketed within a capitalist economy remain an important focus for the study of popular culture.[374] Thus the production aspect of the understanding of the popular is emphasized, but this understanding of production means that 'audience' is undervalued in his work. Adorno's view of those who consume popular culture is deeply pessimistic. Those who consume the products of the culture industry are regarded as passive and largely ignorant of real artistic judgement.[375] Adorno's discussion of popular culture, although it is a critique from the left,

---

370 Adorno, T. W. (1991), *The Culture Industry*, London: Routledge, p. 85.
371 Adorno, *Culture*, p. 85.
372 Adorno, *Culture*, p. 87.
373 Adorno, T. W., 'On Popular Music', in Storey, *Culture*, p. 211.
374 McGuigan, *Cultural*, p. 47.
375 Adorno, *Popular*, p. 211.

can be seen in parallel to the high culture/low culture views associated with Arnold.

What Adorno introduces to the high culture/low culture debate is a critique that views the processes of production in popular culture as inherently suspect. This perspective is taken up in theological discussion of culture. For instance Paul Tillich, while he was at pains to value cultural expression outside the Church, was highly critical of popular culture because it was generated through a culture industry. As Kelton Cobb points out, Tillich was personally close to Adorno and others in the Frankfurt school, and he shared with them a suspicion of all aspects of popular culture. So while he would value high art, such as painting, says Cobb, his 'aversion to popular culture was one constant in Tillich's theology of culture in both its early and later phases'.[376] This notion that the culture industries exercise an undue power over consumers is continued in more recent theological discussion of popular culture, for instance in the work of Kenda Creasey Dean, who argues that the culture industries threaten the moral and spiritual development of young people. [377]

Culture Industry and the Way of Life

The pessimistic view of the impact of the culture industry upon groups and individuals associated with Adorno has been widely contested. In the early development of cultural studies these views were first challenged by Raymond Williams, Richard Hoggart and E. P. Thompson.[378] In *The Long Revolution* Williams develops a social definition of culture: 'the social definition of culture is descriptive of a particular way of life, which expresses certain meanings and values not only in

---

376 Cobb, K. (2005), *The Blackwell Guide to Theology and Popular Culture*, Oxford: Blackwell, p. 97.

377 See Creasey Dean, K. (2004), *Practicing Passion: Youth and the Quest for a Passionate Church*, Grand Rapids: Eerdmans. The view that people are manipulated and duped by the power of advertising and the 'culture industries' continues to hold sway particularly among Christian cultural commentators.

378 See Williams, R. (1958), *Culture and Society 1780–1950*, Harmondsworth: Penguin; Hoggart, R. (1958), *The Uses of Literacy*, London: Penguin; and Thompson, E. P. (1963), *The Making of The English Working Class*, Harmondsworth: Penguin.

art and learning but also in institutions and ordinary behaviour'.[379] What grows from this kind of analysis is what Williams calls a pattern of a 'whole way of life'.[380] Williams describes particular patterns associated with individual cultures and historical periods as a 'structure of feeling'.[381] That culture can be described as a 'whole way of life' or 'structure of feeling' arises essentially from Williams's concern to assert the ordinariness of culture. His argument that culture is 'ordinary' was developed as a reaction to the 'elitist' views of writers such as Adorno and Arnold, and it laid the foundation for the way of seeing that came to be termed cultural studies.[382]

Richard Hoggart's *The Uses of Literacy*[383] deals with the popular culture by exploring the culture of the English working classes. In part a recounting of the lives and behaviour of those among whom he was brought up in the north of England, the book represents this 'culture' as being under threat from what is termed 'mass culture'.

> My argument is not that there was, in England one generation ago, an urban culture still very much 'of the people' and that now there is only a mass urban culture. It is rather that the appeals made by mass publicists are for a great number of reasons made more insistently, effectively, and in a more comprehensive and centralised form today than they were earlier; that we are moving towards the creation of a mass 'culture'; that the remnants of what was at least in parts an urban culture 'of the people' are being destroyed; and that the new mass culture is in some important ways less healthy than the often crude culture it is replacing.[384]

A similar interest in the cultural creativity of the working class is evident in the work of the historian E. P. Thompson. In *The Making of the English Working Class* Thompson argues that the emergence of

---

379 Williams, R. (1965), *The Long Revolution*, Harmondsworth: Penguin, p. 56.

380 Williams, R. (1994 [1961]), 'The Analysis of Culture', in Storey, J. (ed.), *Cultural Theory and Popular Culture: A Reader*, Hemel Hempstead: Harvester Wheatsheaf.

381 Williams, 'Analysis', p. 61.

382 McGuigan, *Cultural*, p. 21; Davies, I. (1995), *Cultural Studies and Beyond: Fragments of Empire*, London: Routledge, p. 16.

383 Hoggart, *Uses*.

384 Hoggart, *Uses*, p. 24.

the working class was an active process in which the people themselves were involved.[385] As Thompson puts it, the working class was 'present at its own making'.[386] Jim McGuigan places Hoggart firmly among the pessimists who denounce mass culture as an erosion of an earlier more authentic working-class urban culture.[387] What Hoggart and Thompson did, however, was to focus attention on the way that communities of ordinary people played a part in creating their own culture. This connects to Williams's idea of culture as a way of life, and so even if Hoggart might be judged to be among the pessimists, his work gave an impetus to the way of seeing that emerged as cultural studies.

For practical theology the insights of Williams and others, that culture is ordinary, and that it is a way of life, are an important corrective to the temptation to dismiss the emergence of a Christian culture industry as inherently corrupting and corrosive of the Church. It corresponds to the way of seeing in cultural studies that views production in relation to both representation and consumption. In other words the meaning of the Christian culture industry is not simply to be read through the action of processes of production: it must also be evaluated by an examination of how theological expression is taken up and made use of by Christian communities as a way of life.

The Practice of Everyday Life

A key issue for practical theology in its evaluation of the Christian culture industry relates to the influence of powerful media-based companies on the shape of the Church. While it is simplistic to dismiss developments in the contemporary Church solely on the basis that they have adopted processes of production that are associated with the culture industry, it is nevertheless true that these processes are powerful and that they have a significant impact not only on the way that theology is circulated but also on the shape of that expression. So this kind of critique must orientate itself in ways that take account of how it is that people make use of the products of the culture industry in everyday life.

---

385 See Thompson, *Making*.
386 Thompson, *Making*, p. 8.
387 McGuigan, *Cultural*, p. 52.

In *The Practice of Everyday Life*[388] de Certeau examines the way that 'users' (or consumers) operate. Consumers, he argues, are often seen as being passive or 'guided by rules'. His work is an attempt to uncover what is hidden by the term consumer; 'the purpose [of this work] is to make explicit the systems of operational combination which also compose "a culture," and to bring to light the models of action characteristic of users whose status as the dominated element in society (a status that does not mean that they are either passive or docile) is concealed by the euphemistic term consumers'.[389] By foregrounding the action of the 'consumer' and the notion of practice de Certeau reframes the relationship to production and the culture industry.

He accepts that 'economy' is culturally dominant but also suggests that consumers are far from manipulated. It is not possible to understand representation simply by describing the intent of its makers, rather the cultural theorist must analyse the way that people use cultural artefacts.[390] In the use of representation, he suggests, there is a making. This production is a kind of *poiesis* (poetic making), 'but a hidden one because it is scattered over areas defined and occupied by systems of "production" (television, urban development, commerce etc.)'.[391] He gives as an example the way that the Spanish colonizers in Latin America imposed their Christian culture on the indigenous Indian peoples. These indigenous groups subverted the culture of the colonizers, not by opposing it, but by using it for their own ends. 'They were other within the very colonization that was outwardly assimilating them.'[392] The indigenous people were not strong enough to challenge the power of the Spanish but they turned this power nevertheless and they escaped without leaving, says de Certeau.[393]

De Certeau explores 'ways of operating'. By this he means the many ways that users re-appropriate the spaces offered by the technologies of cultural production.[394] These re-appropriations are 'microbe-like' and

388 De Certeau, M. (1984), *The Practice of Everyday Life*, trans. Rendell, S., Berkeley: University of California Press.
389 De Certeau, *Practice*, pp. xi–xii.
390 De Certeau, *Practice*, p. xiii.
391 De Certeau, *Practice*, p. xii.
392 De Certeau, *Practice*, p. xiii.
393 De Certeau, *Practice*, p. xiii.
394 De Certeau, *Practice*, p. xiv.

they are characterized by what he calls 'tactics'. Tactics are the ways that the weak win victories over the strong. Tactics involve: 'clever tricks, knowing how to get away with things, "hunter's cunning", manoeuvres, polymorphic simulations, joyful discoveries, poetic as well as warlike'.[395] Thus popular culture emerges as a series of 'arts of making' based around the use and combination of different modes of consumption. These are 'poetic ways of making do'.[396] This kind of subcultural activity is no longer experienced around the edges of society, all popular culture works in this way.

> Marginality is today no longer limited to minority groups, but is rather massive and pervasive; this cultural activity of the non-producers of culture and activity that is unsigned, unreadable and unsymbolised, remains the only one possible for all those who never-the-less buy and pay for the showy products through which a productionist economy articulates itself. Marginality is becoming universal.[397]

So as the stability of society breaks down, says de Certeau, marginality is experienced by increasing numbers of people. Consensus gives way to fragmented nomadic groups. The individual, 'increasingly constrained by vast frameworks detaches himself from them without being able to escape them and can henceforth only try to outwit them, to pull tricks on them'.[398] The individual seeks a kind of rural freedom in the midst of the computerized metropolis. While production may be 'centralised, spectacular and clamorous', de Certeau argues that it is confronted by consumption, which he sees as a different kind of production.[399] Consumption is characterized by ruses, clandestine activity and invisibility. Thus in the practice of everyday life the nature of the subject becomes 'politicized'.[400]

In de Certeau's work the relationship between representation (text), production and consumption (audience) is re-theorized. His work has

---

395 De Certeau, *Practice*, p. xix.
396 De Certeau, *Practice*, p. xv.
397 De Certeau, *Practice*, p. xvii.
398 De Certeau, *Practice*, p. xxii.
399 De Certeau, *Practice*, p. 31.
400 De Certeau, *Practice*, p. xxii.

been influential within cultural studies; in particular it has been taken up in the work of John Fiske.[401] Fiske, like de Certeau, gives weight to the power of the economy. Popular culture is integrally related to an economic system that attempts to recreate itself ideologically in its own commodities.[402] Thus, 'a commodity is an ideology made material'. At the same time commodities, such as denim jeans, can hold a number of meanings, so they have a 'semiotic richness'.[403] The potential for symbolic use of commodities means that the ideological loading of meaning does not have to be accepted. It is possible to create new meanings with the same item, for example ripping the knees out of a brand new pair of Levi jeans creates a new symbolic meaning. Fiske calls this process excorporation: 'Excorporation is the process by which the subordinate make their own culture out of the resources and commodities provided by the dominant system.'[404]

Denied access to a viable 'folk culture', popular culture emerges as the construction of subordinate groups. Popular culture, says Fiske, is made by the people and not by the 'culture industry'. The role of the culture industry is to produce 'a repertoire of texts or cultural resources for the various formations of the people to use or reject in the on going process of producing their popular culture'.[405] The problems of everyday life in complex and varied social structures mean that people have developed 'nomadic subjectivities'. These 'shifting allegiances' allow them to move around, linking with groups where they wish and moving on when they wish.[406] Fiske draws heavily upon de Certeau, arguing that, rather than being regarded as subjugated, individuals should be seen as active agents in a cultural economy. The use of commodities as locations for pleasure and meaning transforms them so that they in turn have a currency and circulation.[407] Thus the study of popular culture should not focus upon products but rather upon the nature of everyday life and how these products find a place in it.

The idea of practice allows de Certeau to address the question of

---

401 Fiske, J. (1989), *Understanding Popular Culture*, London: Routledge.
402 Fiske, *Understanding*, p. 14.
403 Fiske, *Understanding*, p. 5.
404 Fiske, *Understanding*, p. 15.
405 Fiske, *Understanding*, p. 24.
406 Fiske, *Understanding*, p. 24.
407 Fiske, *Understanding*, p. 24.

individual agency in relation to the mediated popular culture dominated by the systems of cultural production. Fiske articulates de Certeau's theoretical framework and relates it to the specifics of cultural production and the semiotics of style in popular culture. For both writers agency is a kind of resistance but it is a resistance within a fragmented and de-centred field of power. The contemporary condition is one where everyone is to some extent marginalized and making do.

Practical Theology and the Christian Culture Industry

Practical theology is the spiritual discipline whereby those in the Church reflect critically on their contemporary forms of expression and practice. The advent of the Christian culture industry is a challenge because it has a tendency to polarize discussion. One of the reasons for this is that the expression of faith in culture means that we are immediately catapulted into the arena of values and taste. As Lawrence Grossberg says, 'culture is the site of the struggle to define how life is lived and experienced, a struggle carried out in the discursive forms available to us. Cultural practices articulate the meanings of particular social practices and events; they define ways we make sense of them, how they are experienced and lived.' [408]

The high culture/low culture debate tends to draw practical theology into precisely these kinds of conflicts. So in seeking to evaluate the Christian culture industry within this debate we are situating theological discussion within the wider culture wars. The notion that culture is a way of life takes this discussion and relocates it in the livedness of communities. With de Certeau and Fiske this move identifies the culture industries as a context in which individuals and communities make use of consumer products to construct their own meanings. Such a move recognizes that the culture industry is powerful and has its own force field of ideology, and yet individuals have their own ways of operating and of making space. A similar process is evident in the contemporary Christian scene. For instance in the way that young people may attend a glitzy charismatic worship event and

---

408 Grossberg, L. (1996), 'On Postmodernism and Articulation: An Interview with Stuart Hall', in Morley, D. and Chen, H. (eds), *Stuart Hall: Critical Dialogues in Cultural Studies*, London: Routledge, pp. 131–50, 158.

yet find space for themselves by texting during the sermon or chatting to their friends during the worship time. The worship leaders and the event organizers could be read as powerful influences on the faith of the younger generation, but this has to be seen through the behaviour and ways of operating of individual young people. So, however powerful and persuasive a large-scale charismatic event may appear to be, there are actually many ways to subvert and make space within these kinds of events. One of the reasons for this is that young people are active in making faith in relation to the Christian culture industry. The products and resources that are generated by the Christian scene may limit choices but they also create opportunities for investment and use as they are animated through the participation of local communities.

Mediation is a muddied arena of cultural expression. For practitioners engaged in reflection on the Church's contextualized expression in popular culture perspectives, the discussion of culture industry drawn from cultural studies can only form a part of an evaluative and critical perspective. They offer frameworks that give what is a partial basis for critique. Participation and mediation are not simply concerned with the cultural expression of faith, they are also related to the way that these processes are divinely indwelt and animated by the Spirit of God. This introduces a theological dynamic in practical theology that calls for constant analysis, critique and constructive comment on the way that the contemporary Church mediates expression. Mediation can be a place of epiphany. Encounter, with God, takes place in the imperfect cultural forms of expression as they are mediated. Yet there is a continual need to examine expression and the practices of mediation to see how these are shaped and formed not only through their cultural circulation but also as places of encounter. To do this kind of critical reflection it is not adequate simply to critique the Christian culture industry on some kind of high culture/low culture basis or because it introduces an inappropriate popularizing tendency into the Christian Church. Neither is it adequate to dismiss the productive processes of the contemporary Christian Church because they are being shaped by the powerful influences of media-based organizations. It is right to be critical of the ways in which the Christian culture industry may be driven, for instance, by the need to generate profit through novelty, or the ways in which it limits expression through the emphasis on particular forms or genres, but this must be balanced by a reading of the cultures of Christian communities. Mediation is a circulation of representation through production and consumption. This means that the theological discussion of mediation as encounter and place for attention and contemplation of Christ must engage with all aspects of mediation.

10

Flow

Flow takes place within the Christian community but it also extends the circulation of representation beyond the boundaries of congregations and denominations. Flow is mediated through the participation of the Christian community. Sharing in flow generates identity and theological capital. At the same time, mediation extends the flow of theological representation into popular culture. This raises questions concerning the relationship between the flow of representation and the way that communities operate as a place of identity formation and difference. If mediation circulates the flow of 'theology' beyond the formal structures of the Church how does this more liquid context relate to participation in a specifically Christian identity? Between flow as it is evidenced in more formal ecclesial structures and the mediation of representation in popular cultures there are ways of being Church that are extended and made fluid. These take the form of networks of communication and belonging that run alongside congregational life and institutional structure. These networks are established and maintained through the flow of theological expression and its mediation in lifestyle and identity.[409] What the networks show are ways of being Church in more fluid ways than the centripetal practice of Church as a taste culture. This last chapter explores the relationship between flow and ecclesial being in these three areas. First, flow within the Christian community and how flow operates as both structure and agency is read through Pierre Bourdieu's theory of practice. Then, the extension of ecclesial being in popular culture is explored through a recording by the country music singer Iris DeMent. Finally, the liquid Church as a networked and permeable form of ecclesial communication is illustrated by a discussion of the Taizé community.

---

409 For more on networks see Ward, P. (2002), *Liquid Church*, Peabody: Henrickson/ Carlisle: Paternoster.

Flow and a Theory of Practice

Pierre Bourdieu's theory of practice sets up a series of relations between what he calls habitus, capital and field. To express this theory, he uses the formula [(habitus) (capital)] + field = practice.[410] This theory of practice can be used to discuss the relationship between structure and agency in the contemporary Church. So the Christian community can be read as operating in similar ways to Bourdieu's understanding of fields of cultural practice. For Bourdieu, field, habitus and capital describe a relationship between social structure and individual agency. Within the Christian community there are similar relations that operate. Participation and mediation describe the action of both individuals and groups in the animation of flow but they also describe a culture that shapes and forms Christians. Participation and flow are therefore both structure and agency. To use Bourdieu's theory of practice, the Church is a field; within this field individuals are shaped, and they embody theology: this is habitus. To operate and manoeuvre within and through the field of the Christian community it is necessary to acquire and make use of theological capital.

Bourdieu uses his conceptual tools of capital, habitus and field to theorize a range of empirically based sociological studies. These include studies of academic life in France, the concept of taste, and what he calls the field of cultural production (or art and literature).[411] In the theory of practice 'field' relates to a series of objective hierarchical relationships between institutions, individuals, texts and discourses. In *The Field of Cultural Production* he describes field as 'the space of literary or artistic position takings'.[412] It is the structuring of these position takings that constitutes the field. 'The literary or artistic field is a *field of forces*, but it is also a *field of struggles* tending to transform or conserve this field of forces.'[413] Within the field, position-taking is defined by what is possible. Each position receives its value in relation

---

410 Bourdieu, P. (1984), *Distinction: A Social Critique of the Judgement of Taste*, trans. Nice, R., London: Routledge, p. 101.

411 Bourdieu, P. (1988), *Homo Academicus*, trans. Collier, P., Cambridge: Polity Press; Bourdieu, *Distinction*; Bourdieu, P. (1993), *The Field of Cultural Production*, ed. and intro. Johnson, R., Cambridge: Polity Press.

412 Bourdieu, *Field*.

413 Bourdieu, *Field*, p. 30.

to the other positions. The positions within the field are flexible and fluid, changing places in relation to one another.[414] The structure of the field, which is what Bourdieu terms 'the space of oppositions', is nothing other than the 'structure of the distribution of the capital of specific properties which governs success in the field and the winning of the external or specific profits (such as literary prestige) which are at stake in the field'.[415]

Capital refers to what is required in order to play in particular fields.[416] Capital is a social relation, which Bourdieu likens to an energy that is produced and reproduced in a particular field:

> In practice, that is in a particular field, the properties, internalized in dispositions or objectified in economic or cultural goods, which are attached to agents are not all simultaneously operative; the specific logic of the field determines those which are valid in this market, which are pertinent and active in the game in question, and which, in the relationship with this field, function as specific capital – and consequently as a factor explaining practice.[417]

There are various kinds of capital. These include educational capital, social capital and cultural capital. These kinds of capital relate to social class in terms of what Bourdieu terms the 'over-all volume of capital'.[418] The distribution of classes therefore runs from those who are provided with most economic and cultural capital to those who are least provided for in these areas. At the same time the total volume of capital conceals how capital might operate in different markets. Capital, says Swartz, is the way that Bourdieu conceptualizes social power. The idea of capital therefore is extended beyond the material, as per Marxism, to include the cultural, the social and the symbolic.[419] So cultural capital is used by Bourdieu to expand the theory of power relations to cultural activities. These may include verbal ability, general

---

414 Bourdieu, *Field*, p. 30.
415 Bourdieu, *Field*, p. 30.
416 Bourdieu, *Distinction*, p. 112.
417 Bourdieu, *Distinction*, p. 113.
418 Bourdieu, *Distinction*, p. 115.
419 Swartz, D. (1997), *Culture and Power: The Sociology of Pierre Bourdieu*, Chicago: University of Chicago Press, p. 73.

cultural awareness, aesthetic preferences, knowledge of the school systems and educational qualifications.[420]

Bourdieu theorizes the interaction between structure and agency as something that is 'active' in the individual. His term for this is habitus. Swartz suggests that Bourdieu is following social constructionists such as Berger and Luckmann in the way that structures are internalized by subjects.[421] Thus habitus both relates to the generation of practices that in turn may be located in an objectively classifiable structure, while at the same time it also relates to the internalized ability to classify practices in the social world.[422] Internalized, the habitus is transformed into a disposition and this disposition in turn generates 'meaningful practices' and 'meaning giving perceptions'.[423] Different conditions produce different habitus. These are generative schemes, which may be transferred from field to field. In these arenas they are perceived as differentiated lifestyles, by those who share the perceptual scheme.[424] So Bourdieu argues that the habitus 'is not only a structuring structure, which organizes practices and the perception of practices, but it is also a structured structure; the principle of division into logical classes which organizes the perception of the social world is itself the product of internalization of the social classes'.[425] Class conditions are described, at the same time, by their intrinsic properties and by their relations within the system of class positions. Thus for Bourdieu class is a system of differences or differential positions. Social identity is defined by everything it is not, and it is thus distinguished by difference.[426] This system of differences is 'inscribed' in the habitus as it is experienced in the life condition of occupying a particular position in the structure. The habitus is a practice-generating scheme that expresses both the necessity and the freedom of a class condition.[427] Against mechanistic interpretations of class consciousness Bourdieu sees habitus as a cognition, yet at the same time against romantic notions

420 Swartz, *Culture*, p. 74.
421 Swartz, *Culture*, p. 97.
422 Bourdieu, *Distinction*, p. 170.
423 Bourdieu, *Distinction*, p. 170.
424 Bourdieu, *Distinction*, p. 115.
425 Bourdieu, *Distinction*, p. 170.
426 Bourdieu, *Distinction*, p. 172.
427 Bourdieu, *Distinction*, p. 172.

of class consciousness he asserts that cognition is based on what he terms a 'misrecognition' or a recognition of an order which is in the mind.[428] Habitus creates a stylistic affinity between individuals of the same class. 'The practices of the same agent, and, more generally, the practices of all agents of the same class, owe the stylistic affinity which makes each of them a metaphor of any of the others to the fact that they are the product of transfers of the same schemes of action from one field to another.'[429]

Preferences (taste), according to Bourdieu, are related to the assertion of 'difference'. Thus in general the affirmation of a particular 'taste' involves the negative refusal of other tastes, and 'nothing more clearly affirms one's class, nothing more infallibly classifies, than taste in music'.[430] 'Objectively and subjectively aesthetic stances adopted in matters of cosmetics, clothing or home decoration are opportunities to experience or assert one's position in social space, as a result of a rank to be upheld or a distance to be kept'.[431] Taste functions socially as 'cultural capital'.[432] Cultural capital is built up by investment and it is worthwhile, because to survive in a given area it can be both necessary, and indeed profitable.[433] Such areas are what Bourdieu calls 'sites of cultural competence'. These sites are places both where cultural competence is produced and where it is given its price. Of course each site attempts to place the highest possible price on the cultural competencies associated with it.

Sarah Thornton makes use of Pierre Bourdieu's theory of taste and practice to interpret dance music and club cultures. [434] Her work is interesting because it gives some clues as to how these highly theoretical categories taken from Bourdieu might be used within practical theology to discuss the contemporary Church. In particular her work is suggestive in that it develops a way of viewing club culture that can be used to describe how the Church through participation and mediation

---

428 Bourdieu, *Distinction*, p. 172.
429 Bourdieu, *Distinction*, p. 173.
430 Bourdieu, *Distinction*, p. 18.
431 Bourdieu, *Distinction*, p. 57.
432 Bourdieu, *Distinction*, p. 85.
433 Bourdieu, *Distinction*, p. 86.
434 Thornton, S. (1995), *Club Cultures*, Cambridge: Polity Press.

operates as a similar kind of taste culture. Thornton argues that the club scene, among British young people, functions as a series of 'taste cultures', that is, it gathers people together on the basis of a shared taste in music and their common consumption of particular media.[435] Thus clubs, she says, act as ad hoc communities. Club culture operates on a crucial distinction between what she calls the 'hip world', and the 'mainstream'. At its heart this distinction is related to 'envisioning social worlds and discriminating between social groups'.[436] She argues that, 'subcultural ideologies are a means by which youth imagine their own and other social groups and affirm that they are not anonymous members of an undifferentiated mass'. 'In this way I am not simply researching the beliefs of a cluster of communities, but investigating the way that they make meaning in "the service of power" – however modest the powers may be.'[437]

To help her in this process, Thornton draws on Bourdieu's theory of cultural capital, arguing, however, that to describe the groups she is studying it is more appropriate to use the term 'subcultural capital'.[438] Subcultural capital, she says, confers status on the holder, and in the eyes of the relevant beholder it can be objectified and embodied: objectified in the artefacts associated with the club scene and embodied in the dances and language that are significant to the club world. Subcultural capital can also be converted into economic capital, for example in the knowledge and hipness of a DJ. So capital operates as a system of value and exchange both within the subculture and between the subculture and those outside the group. Crucial to all this is the role of the media. For Bourdieu the media was significant as a cultural symbol and therefore as a marker of distinction. Thornton argues, however, that the media is a primary factor in the circulation of subcultural capital.[439] 'I would argue that it is impossible to understand the distinctions of youth subcultures without some systematic investigation of their media consumption.'[440] Thus being 'in' or 'out', high or low in

---

435 Thornton, *Club*, p. 3.
436 Thornton, *Club*, p. 5.
437 Thornton, *Club*, p. 10.
438 Thornton, *Club*, p. 11.
439 Thornton, *Club*, p. 13.
440 Thornton, *Club*, p. 13.

subcultural capital, says Thornton, relates in complex ways to 'media coverage, creation and exposure'.[441]

Liquid Church as Practice

Drawing on Bourdieu and Thornton the Church can be seen to operate as a field or a taste culture. Within the field of the Church there is a flow of communication and position-taking. Flow generates theological capital by circulation. Theological capital as it flows through mediation operates as a unit of exchange allowing individuals to function as, say, a minister, as worship leaders, or as members of a congregation. Church as a field consists of a series of roles or positions. The positions (and therefore the field) are made up by the moves of both leaders and members. Flow facilitates these moves. A move may be as simple as preaching a sermon or singing a song. Through participation in the mediation of the flow of theological representation in the field, various positions are constructed. So flow is set in motion within the communication of the community, and facilitates the development of identities and career trajectories. So the Church as field is a structure that emerges from individual and collective agency in relation to the flow of theological representation.

Through participation in the flow of expression individuals are shaped and formed. Sharing in the circulation of the flow of theological representation can therefore be said to develop a Christian habitus. The habitus of the Christian refers to the way that flow is internalized as identity and how this identity is embodied in lifestyle and ethics. Flow therefore structures the habitus as way of life. Participation in the flow of expression develops a specific theological capital. Capital is internalized as part of identity formation, and as habitus it becomes a force that shapes Christian living.

Participation in flow shapes Christian identity, and this identity functions as distinction and difference. Flow and theological capital mark the boundaries of the community. To be Christian therefore is to be part of a church and to participate in the communication of that community. Sharing in communicative practice relates to the circulation of expression and how flow develops both capital and habitus.

---

441 Thornton, *Club*, p. 14.

The Christian lifestyle operates as a structure of theological taste and position-taking both within the community and also in relation to mediation. Thornton's suggestion that the media should be seen as a form of circulation is particularly helpful at this point. In the field of the Church the mediating actions of the contemporary Christian community can be seen to operate in similar ways to the club culture.

The idea of the Church as a field where the flow of representation as it is mediated shapes and forms habitus is highly suggestive. It shows how the cultural practice of mediation functions as both structure and agency in relation to the animation of theological expression. The Church exists as structure because it is a field in which individuals can find a place. These places operate as relationship (or fellowship) but they also generate a pattern or structure of communal relations. Within the structure of the field individuals are actively being Christian and by being active they in turn make the field and its possibilities. Agency, however, is itself structured by the internalization of theological capital and the construction of habitus. So being Christian is an embodied expression of flow. For communities this field of operation is a meaningful place of belonging and identity, but through the freedom of the Spirit it is also a place of animation. Participation in the dynamic relations of the field and habitus of the Christian community is also therefore a sharing in the divine life.

The interpretative categories drawn from Bourdieu offer a way to understand how the Church can be viewed both as a structure where flow operates within communal relationships and as a place where individuals are active agents in relation to this flow. So flow shapes both the possibilities and positions of the community while also forming the habitus of the Christian. Yet there is an important question that arises from this use of field, habitus and capital in relation to the Church. Bourdieu's theory of practice was developed in order to explain the way that individuals, while operating as active agents, tended to reproduce the same social structure as had previously existed. For instance one of the purposes of the theory was to describe how and why it was the case that children passing through the French education system tended to achieve similar results to their parents. So Bourdieu offers an explanation of a fluid movement that is actually rather static or at least that is very slow to change.

Given the radical changes in the contemporary Church this theory of practice may not be the most appropriate interpretative tool. The fluid nature of the Church, I have suggested, is based on movement, circulation and animation, but there is also something in the contemporary Church that is rather static. For while some churches in the UK may be growing, there is not really the kind of dramatic increase as a result of the media-based expression of faith that might at first be expected. So while there may be a flow of mediated expression, this operates almost entirely within the specific field of the Church. While this flow of 'theology' may be meaningful and significant to insiders, it circulates in something of a closed system. On the face of it what has been achieved is that church has become a rather more attractive place for those who already attend. At the same time, through youth ministry and the development of an evangelical subculture, the media-oriented flow of expression has ensured that the children of evangelicals are much more likely to remain within the Christian community – this it should be admitted is no small feat. The contradiction that lies within the success of the contemporary Church is that while it has found ways to mediate faith within a 'taste culture' it has done so by creating heightened difference and distinction. As being inside the flow has become more meaningful it has served to create distance in relation precisely to those people who the Church is called to serve. So the Christian community as a fluid taste culture both includes and excludes.

Flow and Field

It is mediation that extends ecclesial being beyond the specific social relations of the field, that is, the traditional boundaries of the Christian community represented by congregations, parishes and denominations. Through the action of the media theological expression is commodified and circulated. This means that, just as there is a circulation of expression within the Christian community, there is also a flow of 'theology' that is taking place in the wider arena of popular culture. Through the action of the media theological expression is set in motion or animated. This animation functions primarily at the level of representation. So popular culture circulates theological expression in texts, these include song lyrics, classical music, the narrative plot of films, the images in advertising, and so on. The mediated flow of popular culture circulates theological expression in ways that flow beyond the field of the Christian community. As theological representation flows and circulates through mediation there is always the possibility that in the freedom of the Spirit it may become a place of epiphany and encounter. This raises questions in relation to the way that theological capital is generated and habitus formed beyond the field of the institutional Church, and indeed whether and to what extent this is possible. These issues are explored in more depth through a discussion of a recording by Iris DeMent called *Lifeline*.[442]

On the album *Lifeline*, the country singer Iris DeMent delivers stripped-down and passionate renditions of old-time American gospel songs and hymns. These include Fanny Crosby's 'Blessed Assurance' and William Walford's 'Sweet Hour of Prayer'. DeMent introduces the songs in the sleeve notes of the CD through her own family biography. She describes how when times were tough, and life was becoming a little too much, her mother would sit down at the piano and sing these songs. The songs seemed to bring resolution and a calm to her mother. Recently, she tells us, she has herself undergone some bad times, and when she was in the middle of this crisis she called her mother. During the phone call her mother told her what she should do, 'Well Iris!', she said, 'You gotta get to a "pe-yan-a"!' DeMent explains the significance of this advice.

> These songs aren't about religion. At least for me they aren't. They're about something bigger than that. There was an urgency in my mother's voice when she sang that came out of desperation, a great need. When I called her that day and she heard the sinking tone in my voice she did what any compassionate person would do she threw me a lifeline.[443]

Robert Wuthnow's observation that growing numbers of Americans appear to identify themselves as 'spiritual but not religious' and similar insights from David Lyon and Wade Clark Roof, connect with Iris

---

442 Iris DeMent, *Lifeline*, Flariella Records FER–1004.
443 DeMent, *Lifeline*, sleeve notes.

DeMent's use of these spiritual songs outside of a church context.[444] Clearly for her these songs have been disconnected from an immediate ecclesial environment and while her story makes it clear that she may prefer to keep a distance from 'religion' it also offers a tantalizing sense that the transformational impact of the practice of hymn-singing remains somehow still alive and vibrant for her. Indeed it is precisely because these songs offer a 'lifeline' that she wishes to share them with the rest of the world.

Lifeline is an example of the way that Christian expression is being circulated within popular culture. Through this kind of mediation 'theology' is animated beyond the specific field of the Church. These media actions produce articulation whereby the hymns are lifted from one place and relocate in another quite different context. This articulation operates first at the level of representation. Iris DeMent takes evangelical theology inscribed in the hymns and through her performance she connects it to a country music genre and sensibility. One of the ways that this articulation takes place is through the personal note concerning the hymns as a lifeline in the sleeve notes of the CD. This story articulates the specifically Christian theology of the hymns with the country music trope of hope in the context of personal suffering. The songs, she says, change her, but she purposely dislocates this transformation from a formal ecclesial context. Interestingly, the assertion that these songs are not about religion is meant to generate a particular kind of authenticity around them. DeMent appears to be saying that the songs are *more meaningful* precisely because they do not carry any of the church-related religious baggage.

She takes the songs and uses them in her own way. This is a practice of meaning-making outside of doctrinal or institutional constraints and as such it is a kind of textual poaching or poetic making.[445] DeMent is seen to be 'making do' as she articulates these Christian hymns in a context of personal crisis, and through them she finds consolation.

---

444 Wuthnow, R. (1998), *After Heaven: Spirituality in America Since the 1950s*, Berkeley: California University Press, p. 2; see also Lyon, D. (2000), *Jesus in Disneyland: Religion in Postmodern Times*, Cambridge: Polity Press, p. ix; Roof, W. C. (1999), *Spiritual Marketplace: Babyboomers and the Remaking of American Religion*, Princeton: Princeton University Press, pp. 33–5.

445 For textual poaching see Jenkins, H. (1992), *Textual Poachers: Television Fans and Participatory Culture*, London: Routledge.

Through the act of recording she then mediates these songs, along with this relocation, through performance and through her own personal narrative, to those who buy her CD. At the same time the song lyrics continue to carry with them their theological references, even as they are poached and reused. *Lifeline* illustrates how theological expression flows and moves in popular culture. This circulation is dislocated from the field of the congregation but through articulation it is relocated in a different sensibility and authenticity. Through this relocation it is animated in unexpected ways. This raises the question of the extent to which participation in this kind of mediation might be a place of divine encounter. There can be no straightforward answer to this question. We cannot peek into the soul of Iris DeMent and we do not know how the mediated hymns may touch the lives of her listeners. What this kind of mediation does show, however, is that encounter may be a possibility. The reason for this, I think, relates to the kind of transformation that DeMent describes as taking place in her own life and in that of her mother. There is a resonance here with the experience of the Christian community and its practice of hymn-singing. The kind of hopeful renewal and change in orientation that DeMent speaks about finds an echo in the Christian experience of worship. In the context of the Church we accept that these hymns may mediate encounter. Could it not be that when they are sung outside of the field of the Christian community they may also mediate encounter? From what DeMent says this might well be the case.

The implications of this observation are wide-ranging for it seems that through mediation the free Spirit is animating theological expression. This fluid circulation of representation would appear to be extending participation beyond the defined boundaries of the field of the Christian community. Moreover, if we are to accept that the hymns can function as encounter for Iris DeMent, could it be that through mediation they might be similarly animated to the listening audience? Flow is therefore not necessarily confined to the field of relations that is the Church. One of the issues this raises relates to how and to what extent theological capital and habitus might be operating beyond the specific and clear boundaries of the field of practice that is the congregation or local Christian community. My own feeling is that there may wel be limits to the development of faith beyond the Christian community but what seems clear is that through mediation the free Spirit is present to people in ways that challenge a centripetal understanding of the Church and a closed-system approach to 'theology' as a place of encounter and revelation. This aspect of flow represents a missiological challenge for the Christian community. It draws us away from the assumption that flow, as the circulation of theological representation, is limited to a closed ecclesial ecosystem. The fluid animation of 'theology' invites the Church to draw away from communication with and to itself into a much broader conversation that is taking place throughout popular culture. This kind of extension of ecclesial life is testing, but there are examples in the life of the Christian community itself where the flow of representation operates in ways that move between and make permeable ecclesial boundaries and structures. One of these is the remarkable Taizé community.

Taizé as Liquid Church

Once a month, along with tens of thousands of other Christians around the world, I receive an email. It is the newsletter of the Taizé community. The community, which was founded by Brother Roger in the immediate aftermath of the Second World War, takes its name from a tiny French village near Cluny where it started.[446] Since its foundation thousands of young people have visited the community. Every week the community hosts between four and six thousand visitors who come to discuss issues of faith and to join the brothers in their cycle of prayer. As a result of the huge number of visitors, Taizé has been the focus for a network of individuals and churches who identify with the community. The existence of this wider network should not be misinterpreted. Taizé is very clear that the brothers are the community. It doesn't matter how many times someone might visit the village in France or take part in other Taizé-related activities it is not possible to join the 'community' unless you are male and willing to sign up to a lifetime commitment. This includes an agreement to share materially and spiritually, embracing a simple lifestyle, and of course a commit-

---

446 For an account of the origins of the Taizé community, see Balado, J. L. G. (1980), *The Story of Taizé*, Oxford: Mowbray.

ment to celibacy. Despite these conditions, for a religious community based in Europe, Taizé, with approximately one hundred brothers, is remarkably buoyant. Yet while so few actually become monks, hundreds of thousands of people have been able to participate in the life of the community.

Taizé is characterized by its distinctive form of prayer. Three times a day all work, discussion groups and Bible studies come to an end and people gather to pray and sing with the brothers. One of the Taizé brothers describes this pattern of prayer:

> The bells call everyone to the church for prayer. Hundreds, sometimes thousands of young adults from many different countries across the world pray and sing with the brothers of the community. Short songs sung over and over again that, in a few words, express a basic reality, quickly grasped by the mind. Then the Bible is read in several languages. At the center of every prayer service, a long moment of silence offers an irreplaceable opportunity to encounter God.[447]

The songs used at Taizé consist of short meditative lyrics set to simple folk tunes. These chants are repeated over and over as an aid to prayer and contemplation. The Bible readings consist of a short section usually from the Psalms that is chanted with a refrain. After the psalm a short, one- or two-line, sentence from the Bible is read. There then follows an extended period of silence. After the silence come the intercessions or what is called 'The litany of prayer'. The litany is described by one of the brothers:

> A prayer composed of short petitions or acclamations, sustained by humming, with each petition followed by a response sung by all, can form a kind of 'pillar of fire' at the heart of the prayer. Praying for others widens our prayer to the dimensions of the entire human family; we entrust to God the joys and the hopes, the sorrows and the sufferings of all people, particularly those who are forgotten. A prayer of praise enables us to celebrate all that God is for us.[448]

447 http://www.taize.fr/en_article3148.html accessed 25 June 2007.
448 http://www.taize.fr/en_article3148.html accessed 25 June 2007.

The service comes to a close with a lengthy period where more songs, again written by the brothers, are sung.

Taizé was founded as an ecumenical community. Instead of adopting a liturgy from a particular church it has produced its own form of prayer. The prayer is a particular expression or representation. The expression of the community can be read as text within the context of the life and worship at Taizé, but it is itself mediated as flow through its production and reproduction in various media-based formats. Taizé encourages those who have visited the community to continue to pray using the songs and the form of prayer developed by the brothers. The Taizé website gives detailed advice on planning and setting up Taizé prayer. This includes advice on making a meditative space and on the way that the songs should be arranged and sung. To help people reproduce Taizé prayer in their local context a series of publications have been produced by the community, including Taizé song books and CDs of the songs, and they also produce recordings of the songs as music-only tracks to enable groups with limited musical resources to sing them in the style of Taizé. As well as the music books and CDs the community also markets DVDs which show the prayer times and also interviews with Brother Roger, it is also possible to buy full-scale reproductions of the Icon of Christ which forms a central focus for the worship. There are also a wide range of books and other material produced by the brothers at Taizé. All of these resources are published in all the European and some non-European languages. As well as the regular email communication, the network of contacts is maintained by the brothers through the regular 'Letter from Taizé'. There are also a number of regional and international gatherings where the brothers lead prayer times. To further facilitate the network each country is assigned an individual brother who visits from time to time. Each year a number of organized visits are planned by denominational and diocesan groups. The brother acts as a contact person within the community for those planning these visits.

The expression of the Taizé community, through its performance in the times of prayer, the hosting of visitors, and in the various media-based publications, is 'set in motion'. The cultural activities of the community 'animate' and enact their embodied theology. This animation flows and is relocated through mediation in the identities, agency and the expression of local communities. With Taizé it is clear that expression is generated or produced from the lived context of the community of brothers, and this is animated in the particular experience of those who visit the community and participate in the programme of prayer, work and discussion. Participation in a visit is part of the circulation of representation within Taizé. Through participation the visitors are active in animating the expression of the brothers. There is a flow of theological expression as individuals and groups take up and embody in social relations the expression of the community mediated through the prayer and the songs.

The flow of representation seen in the activity of the Taizé community develops a complex interaction between communities, media, texts and identity. Circulation is particularly evident in the prayer and singing of the community. In the prayer, representation is sonically animated. The songs create an environment which itself is lived in and also indwelt. At the most basic level individuals participate in the prayer by singing. They create the environment by making sound with their bodies. Song is inside them, indwells them, but it also surrounds them and they dwell in the soundscape they themselves have created. The sound is animated, enacted as it is performed. It is an embodied practice where texts in performance circulate. As they circulate they are lived in through participation. The Taizé chants are simultaneously made up of music and lyrics. The song lyrics are short theological phrases. These phrases are particular representations of an aspect of faith. For instance the song 'Jesus remember me' has the simple lyric 'Jesus remember me, when you come into your kingdom'. The lyric is taken from the words of one of the two criminals crucified with Jesus (Luke 23.42). The lyric speaks of the kingdom located in the future, but this is articulated with a personal present. The kingdom is connected to personal prayer and contemplation. In the lyric the singer is positioned in a particular conversation by the direct request: 'remember me'. In the Gospel Jesus responds to the criminal with these words, 'Truly I tell you, today you will be with me in Paradise' (Luke 23.43). This response does not form part of the lyric yet it is implicit in the request. It is in performance that this conversation can be completed. The text sets up this enacted and embodied encounter. The lyrics of the song are enacted as they are sung. This is a conversation, which

183

is not just lived in but is also indwelt by the divine response. Circulation therefore also relates to the way animated texts in performance mediate embodied encounter with the divine.

When it is performed in worship the song is repeated or circulated at some length. Singing in this form sets these theological ideas in motion. They circulate sonically. The form of the song creates a space where the lyric is formed and made by people using their bodies to make the sound. The lyrics are shaped by vocalization but they also act on the body as a sonic environment. The repetition of the melody and the lyric marks time. The singing creates a temporal period of time or space in which prayer and contemplation can be entered into. Prayer becomes a kind of constructed environment of circulation where theological representation is formed and animated. Like a room filled with snow or feathers the circulation in the prayer is a moving fluid space of circulating representation. This is an animated space but it is also a space in which those who participate can rest and abide.

The idea of circulation and flow can be extended to the wider mediations of the Taizé community. The newsletters, email communication, website, books, organized visits, local prayer, and so on are also forms of mediated and fluid circulation. They too are places where representation is animated and circulates. As they are taken up and embodied by individuals and groups they are set in motion as places to live in. The cultural expression and mediation of Taizé therefore operates as an animated and fluid theological environment. Sharing in this lived-in cultural expression is not simply a cultural expression of faith, it is also a place where circulation is indwelt by God. Circulation in the prayer times and through the other forms of communication and networking used by the Taizé community mediate divine encounter as flow.

From the earliest writings of Brother Roger and on to the present, Taizé have sought to encourage an ecumenical vision of reconciliation between churches and religious communities alongside a passionate commitment to the poor and dispossessed. Transformation is a reference to the way that circulation mediates or transmits this vision for the Church. Transformation is mediated through circulation indirectly. There is no direct connection or organizational intentionality among the brothers. Transformation takes place as individuals and groups are taken up, inhabited, and inhabit the flow of cultural circulation. Participation in the circulation of the Taizé community animates and effects transformation producing theological capital and Christian habitus. At the same time this lived-in mediated sphere is also indwelt. Transformation does not solely consist in socialization or cultural competence. It is in turn animated by the presence of God.

The divine presence flows as mediation within the times of prayer with their singing, Bible reading and prayer, but it is also mediated in the wider communicative, social and media-based practices around the Taizé community. Mediation enables transformation to be extended beyond the small village in Burgundy. Mediation effects an ongoing transformative fluid circulation for individuals and communities. Here the activity of the community in producing texts and products becomes a vital means whereby transformation can be enacted beyond the times of prayer. It is through these mediating relationships between the inscribed meanings in the texts produced and mediated by the Brothers and the extended network associated with the community, and the ways in which these meanings find a location in enacted and embodied transformation in the lives of individuals and communities, that circulation becomes flow. Flow suggests that circulation is not turned in upon itself. Flow connects mediation to the animation of the Spirit. Flow relates to transformation as participation in the divine life, the Trinitarian mission of God.

Liquid Church: Mediation and the Extension of Ecclesial Being

Communion with God, as Zizioulas says is not a practice of the Church, rather it is communion which constitutes the Church. [449] Mediation extends this encounter and as it does so it liquifies ecclesial life. Zizioulas imagines communion and the Eucharist in fairly defined and predetermined ecclesial ways. As we have already seen, the default setting in the contemporary theological discussion of the Trinity and the Church tends to be the field of the local congregation as it is gathered around the Eucharist. When this centripetal

---

449 Zizioulas, J. (1985), *Being as Communion: Studies in Personhood and the Church*, Crestwood, NY: Saint Vladimir's Seminary Press, p. 81. See also Ward, *Liquid*.

inclination is articulated with an implied critique of individualism and modernity there can be a tendency to eschew or bracket out the aspects of contemporary ecclesial practice which orientate around the use of the media.

The Taizé community illustrates the extent to which, in the current practices of the contemporary Church, relations and expression are shifting in the flow of a mediated culture. The fluid mediation of expression lifts encounter and transformation from the closed circuit represented by the specific field of the Christian community. Taizé is particularly significant in this respect because it is located outside the regulation of any single ecclesial body. As an ecumenical religious community it is in relationship with a number of ecclesial bodies but it is institutionally independent. Yet through mediation its particular expression flows through and within the more formal field of ecclesial communities. While it has remained outside denominational structures, Taizé has managed to achieve a significant level of recognition and acceptance in European Church life. In his lifetime Brother Roger was supported and embraced by successive Popes, Archbishops of Canterbury and countless other church leaders. From its beginnings a great many theologians have made their own journeys to this small village in rural France. In short it is widely accepted as 'a good thing' to use the terminology of *1066 and All That*.[450]

Taizé is accepted by many of us within the theological community. As I have said, it is highly likely that, like me, many theologians and church leaders may have visited the community and valued the experience. In other words I am trying to draw the reader into a reflexive reading of Taizé. Reflexive in that it is a self-conscious reading of the participant and the insider: faith seeking understanding. At the same time I am trying to make the innovative connection between this experience and the ideas of circulation and flow as part of the extension of ecclesial life. Taizé challenges the assumption that theological capital and the Christian habitus are only generated within congregational settings. Those who have visited the community, sung the song, and so

---

450 Sellar, W. C. and Yeatman, R. J. (1930), *1066 and All That: A Memorable History of England, comprising All the Parts you can Remember, including 103 Good Things, 5 Bad Kings and 2 Genuine Dates*, London: Methuen.

on, have shared in what is a more fluid form of ecclesial life. As participants we have lived in the cultural expression of the community, we have been active in its circulation. So in Taizé we have already shared in an extended ecclesial life where circulation has been animated, lived in and indwelt.

Taizé is a long way from new developments in ecclesial life such as alternative worship, the charismatic movement, Fresh Expressions or the Emerging Church, but it shares with them the extension of ecclesial being through mediation. Taizé is interesting because it demonstrates the extent to which mediation characterizes aspects of the very wide range of ecclesial practice. So the liquid Church is really not that strange. Through Taizé we may begin to recognize that even those of us who are committed to more traditional forms of church may have occasionally dipped our toe in water. Taizé is therefore an example of a more fluid form of church. It is liquid in the way that it connects networks of Christians through mediation. The circulation of representation animates this liquid flow of relationship and divine communion. At the same time Taizé is explicitly committed to the existing life, traditions and institutions of the churches while it also seeks to bring about a renewal and effect change. It shows how theological capital is mediated and flows beyond the specific field of congregational life. The flow of expression seen in Taizé demonstrates how the field of ecclesial life is permeable. Mediation allows Taizé to operate in a fluid manner through a shift in patterns of transformation as the circulation of representation is animated in the embodied belonging and identity of those who participate in the cultural expression of the community. Mediation is a means whereby the ecclesial being is extended and made more fluid. In Taizé we see the way that cultural/theological expression and the circulation of products situates belonging, encounter and transformation in a more fluid and diverse way than the field of the local church. Through participation in this flow, divine being or communion is extended and made more fluid. The life of God is mediated beyond the walls and indeed the social relations of the congregation. This is a liquid Church. In the field of the traditional Church, 'theology' circulates as expression within existing social patterns. In the network established by fluid mediation connectivity follows the circulation of representation as identities are relocated in mediation.

Distinction and Flow in the Liquid Church

Through mediation Christian doctrine is seen to flow beyond the formal structures of the field of the Church. There are interconnecting discourses that coexist. In the Church, doctrine circulates through the practices of believers, but it is equally important that practical theology is able to take note of the various ways that doctrine is also animated in the mediation of popular culture. In the formal church setting theological capital and habitus shape a culture of distinction. Insiders are defined and shaped through practice. They occupy positions and exercise influence and gain significance through their acquired theological capital. There are social rewards in the form of belonging, identity and difference in being Christian. In the contemporary church scene there has developed a strong subculture based on the production, circulation and consumption of particular forms of representation. Being Christian, the Christian habitus, has been strengthened and developed though these mediations. Adopting the forms of communication used in popular culture has shaped the contemporary Church as a place of significance and identity. The combination of the rise in mediation and the identification of believers with the Church as a communal place of belonging means that the Church has effectively become a kind of taste culture in the context of other taste cultures. This taste culture operates as distinction and difference. The success of much of contemporary church life rests on the attractiveness of this difference. To insiders the Church is a place of refuge and safety.

The practice of faith involves communities in the circulation of representation. In the Eucharist, preaching, fellowship, identity and lifestyle, doctrine is set in motion and flows. The agency of individuals animates representations. This animation and motion shapes a world of meaning for the believers. To believe is to be in the flow and to participate in its animation. Capital relates to the ability to produce and circulate representation. The creation of expression and the movement of that expression in communal life animates faith for individuals and for communities. This circulating cultural expression and performance becomes a place of divine encounter as the agency of believers is in turn animated by the Spirit.

Being in the flow and animated by the life of God acts as difference and distinction for the Christian community. The subculture is legitimated by divine encounter. For believers the field of the traditional Church is a place of the divine presence. In the communal practices of prayer, preaching and the Eucharist God is experienced as epiphany. So to be part of the flow is to be part of the 'people of God'. The attractional understanding of mission rests on this assumption. People should and will come to church because it is a diverting subcultural world but it is also a place where they can meet with God. The Emerging Church and Fresh Expressions of church have largely understood mission in this context as attraction and difference. Their strategy has been to reframe belonging around cultural expression: the coffee bar church, or the church in a school, or the church that meets in small groups (cell church), youth church, or the church that uses dance music. For those who have joined these kinds of churches the fresh expression has become a place of significance. It is an adjustment in the subcultural mediated culture of evangelicalism but its purpose is to build community. The community rests on difference and socially it acts as capital and distinction. In these new forms of church the basic dynamic of flow still operates as a field. For those who choose to belong it generates theological capital and habitus through participation. What these new ecclesial forms have not so far done is find ways to engage with theological expression as it is mediated in popular culture. So while we may see aspects of a liquid Church in fresh expression, just as it is there in the field of regular church life, and in the more extended networks represented by the Taizé community, these forms of circulation run the risk of being self-referential and centripetal ecosystems. So while theological representation may be circulating in Fresh Expressions it generally flows between those who are insiders to the field of the Church.

Flow and the Mission of God

Mediation has been widely adopted by the contemporary Church. Communication technology has generated a subcultural scene where representation and performance are flows within local and congregational boundaries. So to be a charismatic Christian is to participate in the flow of products and expression that circulates through the global networks. Similar dynamics are seen to be at play in a more traditional church setting, for instance where communication technology has meant that Anglicans can engage in a global debate concerning theology, practice and identity. Mediation, however, is not confined to the Church. At the same time as the Church is reframing itself as a taste culture, theological representation is also circulating and being animated in popular culture through the processes of mediation. In music, movies, plays, novels, advertisements, therapeutic practices, gardening, and so on, theological expression is in play. This means that through mediation theological representation is circulating beyond the specific confines of the field of the Church. This raises issues for the nature of mission and the shape of ecclesial belonging.

A central missiological issue for the Western Church relates to how it chooses to react to the mediation of the spiritual in popular culture. The attractional Church has responded by adopting the communication technologies of mediation. It has thereby transformed itself into a subcultural expression of communal life. This functions as field of position-taking and place for the circulation of expression as capital. Yet as one taste culture situated among others the contemporary Christian community is faced with the missiological contradiction of difference and distinction. The challenge lies in finding ways to transcend its success in generating and circulating theological capital through and within its own community of practice. The mediation of theological representation in popular culture is evidence that theological expression is in some sense still seen as holding significance and meaning. This is why Iris DeMent can sing Christian hymnody and still find that it is a lifeline. The personal God cannot be seen as distant or removed or indifferent to such a song. Epiphany may be made more common through mediation. It is likely that epiphany may lead to contemplation and this may generate theological capital and habitus but this will most likely take place outside the centripetal ecosystem of the Church as field.

This takes us back to where this journey in practical theology first started. For just as the young people that I was working with in Oxford were starting to develop faith outside of formal ecclesial structures, what we see in the way that theological expression is mediated in popular culture is that participation flows beyond the current patterns of

Church. I would include in this observation all of the new forms of attractional models of Christian community represented by the Emerging Church and Fresh Expressions. This means that the new forms of Christian community are at risk of finding themselves to be just as redundant as more traditional forms of ecclesial life when it comes to finding a way of missionally interacting with the flow of 'theology' in popular culture. The mediation of theological expression in popular culture represents a vital and urgent missional challenge. How can theological capital and the Christian habitus be developed in this context of an extended ecclesial life? This is a complicated issue and will require further reflection that lies beyond the framework of this book. What seems clear is that the mediation of the divine life that has allowed the Christian community to extend and make more fluid its ecclesial being, suggests that such an enterprise may indeed be possible. The clue to the way forward lies in the freedom of God to be present both in the Church and beyond it through participation and mediation. So like a light beckoning us forward the Spirit is inviting us to find a way to 'go with the flow' of the liquid Church.

Bibliography

Adorno, T. W. (1991), *The Culture Industry*, London: Routledge

Adorno, T. W. (1994), 'On Popular Music', in Storey, J. (ed.), *Cultural Theory and Popular Culture: A Reader*, Hemel Hempstead: Harvester Wheatsheaf

Amannaki Havea, S. (1987), *South Pacific Theology*, Oxford: Regnum Books

Anselm (1974), 'Proslogion' in Hopkins, J. and Richardson, H. W. (trans.), *Anselm of Canterbury*, vol. 1, London: SCM Press

Arbuckle, G. (1990), *Earthing the Gospel: An Inculturation Handbook for Pastoral Workers*, London: Geoffrey Chapman

Archbishops' Council (2000), *Common Worship*, London: Church House Publishing

Archbishops' Council (2004), *Mission Shaped Church: Church Planting and Fresh Expressions of Church in a Changing Context*, London: Church House Publishing

Arnold, M. (1869), *Culture and Anarchy* (1932 edn), Cambridge: Cambridge University Press

Athanasius (1891), *Incarnation of the Word*, in *A Select Library of the Nicene and Post-Nicene Fathers of the Christian Church*, edited by Philip Schaff, Second Series, vol. 4: *St Athanasius: Select Works and Letters*, Oxford: Parker

Athanasius (1944), *St Athanasius on the Incarnation*, translated by a religious of CSMV, London: Mowbray

Balado, J. L. G. (1980), *The Story of Taizé*, Oxford: Mowbray

Ballard, P. and Pritchard, J. (1996), *Practical Theology in Action: Christian Thinking in the Service of Church and Society*, London: SPCK

Barker, C. (2000), *Cultural Studies: Theory and Practice* (2nd edn), London: Sage

Barrett, C. K. (1973), *A Commentary on The Second Letter to the Corinthians*, London: A & C Black

Barth, K. (1957), 'Theology and Mission in the Present', trans. Nigrelli, D., in Thomas, N. (ed.), (1995), *Readings in World Mission*, London: SPCK

Barth, K. (1960), *Anselm: Fides Quaerens Intellectum*, trans. Robertson, I. N., London: SCM Press

Barth, K. (1975), *Church Dogmatics* I/1 (2nd edn), trans. Bromiley, G. W. and Torrance, T. F., Edinburgh: T & T Clark

Baumann, Z. (2000), *Liquid Modernity*, Cambridge: Polity Press

Bennington, J. (1973), *Culture, Class and Christian Beliefs*, London: Scripture Union

Bevans, S. (2002), *Models of Contextual Theology* (2nd edn), Maryknoll: Orbis

Bloom, A. (1971), *School for Prayer*, London: DLT

Bosch, D. (1992), *Transforming Mission: Paradigm Shifts in Theology of Mission*, Maryknoll: Orbis

Bourdieu, P. (1984), *Distinction: A Social Critique of the Judgement of Taste*, trans. Nice, R., London: Routledge

Bourdieu, P. (1988), *Homo Academicus*, trans. Collier, P., Cambridge: Polity Press

Bourdieu, P. (1993), *The Field of Cultural Production*, ed. and intro. Johnson, R., Cambridge: Polity Press

Browning, D. (1991), *A Fundamental Practical Theology: Descriptive and Strategic Proposal*, Minneapolis: Fortress Press

Browning, D. (2000), 'Pastoral Theology in a Puralistic Age', in Woodward, J. and Pattison, S. (eds), *The Blackwell Reader in Pastoral and Practical Theology*, Oxford: Blackwell, p. 93

Calvin, J. (1964), *The Second Epistle of Paul to the Corinthians and the Epistles of Timothy, Titus and Philemon*, trans, Smail, T. A., Grand Rapids: Eerdmans

Cartledge M. (2003), *Practical Theology: Charismatic and Empirical Perspectives*, Carlisle: Paternoster

Cassell, B. (1999), 'WWJD', *Group Magazine*, March/April

Cobb, K. (2005), *The Blackwell Guide to Theology and Popular Culture*, Oxford: Blackwell

Cone, J. (1972), *The Spirituals and Blues*, New York: Seabury Press

Cray G. (2004), *From Here to Where? The Culture of the Nineties*, Board of Mission Occasional Papers, 3, London: Board of Mission

Creasey Dean, K. (2004), *Practicing Passion: Youth and the Quest for a Passionate Church*, Grand Rapids: Eerdmans

Cunningham, D. S. (1998), *These Three are One: The Practice of Trinitarian Theology*, Oxford: Blackwell

Davies, I. (1995), *Cultural Studies and Beyond: Fragments of Empire*, London: Routledge

De Certeau, M. (1984), *The Practice of Everyday Life*, trans. Rendall, S., Berkeley: University of California Press

Donovan, V. (1978), *Christianity Rediscovered: An Epistle From the Masai*, London: SCM Press

Dragas, G. (1980), *The Meaning of Theology: An Essay in Greek Patristics*, Darlington: Darlington Carmel

Du Gay, P., Hall, S., Janes, L., Mackay, H. and Negus, K. (1997), *Doing Cultural Studies: The Story of the Sony Walkman*, London: Sage

Enroth, R. M., Ericson, E. E. and Peters, C. B. (1972), *The Story of the Jesus People: A Factual Survey*, Exeter: Paternoster Press

Farley, E. (1983), *Theologia: The Fragmentation and Unity of Theological Education*, Philadelphia: Fortress Press

Fee, G. (1994), *God's Empowering Presence: The Holy Spirit in the Letters of Paul*, Peabody: Hendrickson

Fiddes, P. (2000), *Participating in God: A Pastoral Doctrine of the Trinity*, London: DLT

Fiske, J. (1989), *Understanding Popular Culture*, London: Routledge

Ford, D. (ed.) (2006), *The Modern Theologians*, (3rd edn), Oxford: Blackwell

Frei, H. (1992), *Types of Christian Theology*, New Haven: Yale University Press

Gelder, K. and Thornton, S. (eds.) (1997), *The Subcultures Reader*, London; Routledge

Gilmour, M. J. (ed.), (2005), *Call Me the Seeker: Listening to Religion in Popular Music*, London: Continuum

Gorringe, T. (2004), *Furthering Humanity: A Theology of Culture*, Aldershot: Ashgate

Graham, E. (1996), *Transforming Practice: Pastoral Theology in an Age of Uncertainty*, London: Mowbray

Graham, E. (2000), 'Practical Theology as Transforming Practice', in Woodward, J. and Pattison, S. (eds), *The Blackwell Reader in Pastoral and Practical Theology*, Oxford: Blackwell

Graham, E., Walton, H. and Ward, F. (2005), *Theological Reflection: Methods*, London: SCM Press

Graham, E., Walton, H. and Ward, F. (2007), *Theological Reflection: Sources*, London: SCM Press

Greeve Davaney, S. (2001), 'Theology and the Turn to Cultural Analysis', in Brown, D., Greeve Davaney, S. and Tanner, K. (eds), *Converging on Culture: Theologians in Dialogue with Cultural Analysis and Criticism*, Oxford: AAR/Oxford University Press

Grossberg, L. (1996), 'On Postmodernism and Articulation; an Interview with Stuart Hall', in Morley, D. and Chen, H. (eds), *Stuart Hall: Critical Dialogues in Cultural Studies*, London: Routledge

Hall, S. and Jefferson, T. (eds.) (1975), *Resistance Through Rituals: Youth Subcultures in Post-war Britain*, London: Hutchinson

Healy, N. (2000), *Church, World and the Christian Life*, Cambridge: Cambridge University Press

Hebdige, D. (1979), *Subculture: The Meaning of Style*, London: Methuen

Hoggart, R. (1958), *The Uses of Literacy*, London: Penguin

Holloway, R. (1993), 'An Outsider's Perspective', in France, R. T. and McGrath, A. E. (eds), *Evangelical Anglicans: Their Influence in the Church Today*, London: SPCK

Howard, R. (1996), *The Rise and Fall of the Nine O'Clock Service*, London: Mowbray

Hughes, P. (1962), *Paul's Second Epistle to the Corinthians*, NICNT, Grand Rapids: Eerdmans

Hunsberger, G. R. (2002), 'The Church in the Postmodern Transition', in Foust, T. F., Hunsberger, G. R., Kirk, A. and Ustorf, W. (eds), *A Scandalous Prophet: The Way of Mission after Newbigin*, Grand Rapids: Eerdmans

Jenkins, H. (1992), *Textual Poachers: Television Fans and Participatory Culture*, London: Routledge

Johnson, R., Chambers, D., Rahuram, P. and Tincknell, E. (2004), *The Practice of Cultural Studies*, London: Sage

Kendrick, G. (1992), *Shine Jesus Shine*, Milton Keynes: Word Books

Kendrick, G. (2001), *Behind the Songs*, Stowmarket: Kevin Mayhew

Kendrick, G., Coates, G., Forster, R. and Green, L. (1992), *March for Jesus*, Eastbourne: Kingsway

Kim, K. (2000), 'Post-modern Mission a Paradigm Shift in David Bosch's Theology of Mission?', in Yates, T. (ed.), *Mission – and Invitation to God's Future*, Sheffield: Cliff College

Kirk, A. (1999), *What is Mission? Theological Explorations*, London: DLT

Kraft, C. H. (1979), *Christianity in Culture*, Maryknoll: Orbis

Kraft, C. H. (1984), *Anthropology for Christian Witness*, Maryknoll: Orbis

Kraft, C. H. and Wisley, T. (eds.) (1979), *Readings in Dynamic Indigeneity*, Pasadena: William Carey Library

Lindbeck, G. (1984), *The Nature of Doctrine*, London: SPCK

Lindberg, C. (1996), *The European Reformations*, Oxford: Blackwell

Lindsey, H. (1970), *The Late Great Planet Earth*, Grand Rapids: Zondervan

Longhurst, B. (1995), *Popular Music and Society*, Cambridge: Polity Press

Luzbetak, L. J. (1988), *The Church and Cultures: New Perspectives in Missiological Anthropology*, Maryknoll: Orbis

Lynch, G. (2005), *Understanding Theology and Popular Culture*, Oxford: Blackwell

Lyon, D. (2000), *Jesus in Disneyland: Religion in Postmodern Times*, Cambridge: Polity Press

BIBLIOGRAPHY

McDannell, C. (1995), *Material Christianity: Religion and Popular Culture in America*, New Haven: Yale University Press

McGuigan J. (1992), *Cultural Populism*, London: Routledge

Milbank, J. (1990), *Theology and Social Theory: Beyond Secular Reason*, Oxford: Blackwell

Miller, D. E. (1997), *Reinventing American Protestantism: Christianity in the New Millennium*, Berkeley: University of California Press

Miller, T. (ed.) (2001), *A Companion to Cultural Studies*, Oxford: Blackwell

Miller, V. J. (2004), *Consuming Religion*, London: Continuum

Mizruchi, S. (2001), *Religion and Cultural Studies*, Princeton: Princeton University Press

Morgan, D. (1998), *Visual Piety: A History and Theory of Popular Religious Images*, Berkeley: University of California Press

Morley, D. and Chen, H. (1996), *Stuart Hall: Critical Dialogues in Cultural Studies*, London: Routledge

Negus, K. (1996), *Popular Music in Theory: An Introduction*, Cambridge: Polity Press

Newbigin, L. (1983), *The Other Side of 1984: Questions for the Churches*, Geneva: World Council of Churches

Newbigin, L. (1989), *The Gospel in a Pluralist Society*, London: SPCK

Nida, E. (1954), *Customs, Culture and Christianity*, London: Tyndale Press

Niebuhr, R. H. (1951), *Christ and Culture*, New York: Harper & Row

Olson, R. E. and Hall C. A. (2002). *The Trinity*, Grand Rapids: Eerdmans

O'Sullivan, T., Hartley, J., Saunders, D., Montgomery, M. and Fiske J. (1994), *Key Concepts in Communication and Cultural Studies*, London: Routledge

Paul VI (1975), *Evangelii Nuntiandi*, Vatican: Sacred Congregation for Evangelization

Price, L. (2002), 'Churches and Postmodernity: Opportunity for Attitude Shift', in Foust, T. F., Hunsberger, G. R., Kirk, A. and Ustorf, W. (eds), *A Scandalous Prophet: The Way of Mission after Newbigin*, Grand Rapids: Eerdmans

Reed, J. (1996), *Glorious Battle: The Cultural Politics of Victorian Anglo-Catholicism*, London: Tufton Books

Riddell, M. (1998), *The Threshold of the Future: Reforming the Church in the Post-Christian West*, London: SPCK

Roberts, P. (1999), *Alternative Worship in the Church of England*, Nottingham: Grove Books

Rojek, C. (2007), *Cultural Studies*, Cambridge: Polity Press

Roof, W. C. (1999), *Spiritual Marketplace: Babyboomers and the Remaking of American Religion*, Princeton: Princeton University Press

Samuel, V. and Sugden, C. (eds.) (1999), *Mission as Transformation: A Theology of the Whole Gospel*, Oxford: Regnum Books

Sanneh, L. (1991), *Translating the Message: The Missionary Impact on Culture*, Maryknoll: Orbis

Scharen, C. (2005), '"Judicious Narratives", or Ethnography as Ecclesiology', *Scottish Journal of Theology* 58(2), pp. 125–42

Schreiter, R. J. (1985), *Constructing Local Theologies*, London: SCM Press

Sellar, W. C. and Yeatman, R. J. (1930), *1066 and All That: A Memorable History of England, comprising All the Parts you can Remember, including 103 Good Things, 5 Bad Kings and 2 Genuine Dates*, London: Methuen

Shorter, A. (1988), *Toward a Theology of Inculturation*, London: Geoffrey Chapman

Shuker, R. (1994), *Understanding Popular Music*, London: Routledge

Sjogren, P. (1975), *The Jesus Prayer*, trans. Linton, S., London: SPCK

Small, C. (1987), *Music of the Common Tongue*, London: Calder Riverrun

Smith, M. J. (2000), *Culture, Reinventing the Social Sciences*, Milton Keynes: Open University Press

Storey, J. (ed.) (1994), *Cultural Theory and Popular Culture: A Reader*, Hemel Hempstead: Harvester Wheatsheaf

Swartz, D. (1997), *Culture and Power: The Sociology of Pierre Bourdieu*, Chicago: University of Chicago Press

Swinton, J. and Mowat, H. (2006), *Practical Theology and Qualitative Research*, London: SCM Press

Tanner, K. (1997), *Theories of Culture*, Minneapolis: Fortress Press

Thompson, E. P. (1963), *The Making of The English Working Class*, Harmondsworth: Penguin

Thornton, S. (1995), *Club Cultures*, Cambridge: Polity Press

Tillich, P. (1951), *Systematic Theology*, vol. 1, Chicago: University of Chicago Press

Tipton, S. M. (1982), *Getting Saved From the Sixties*, Berkeley: University of California Press

Torrance, A. (1996), *Persons in Communion: Trinitarian Description and Human Participation*, Edinburgh: T & T Clark

Tracy, D. (1975), *Blessed Rage for Order: The New Pluralism in Theology*, Chicago: University of Chicago Press

Tracy, D. (1981), *The Analogical Imagination*, London: SCM Press

Van der Ven, J. (1990), *Practical Theology and Empirical Approach*, trans. Schultz, B., Kampen: Peeters

Verstraelen, F. J. (1996), 'Africa in David Bosch's Missiology: Survey and Proposal', in Saayman, W. and Kritzinger, K. (eds), *Mission in Bold Humility: David Bosch's Work Considered*, Maryknoll: Orbis

Volf, M. (1996), *Exclusion and Embrace*, Nashville: Abingdon Press

Volf, M. (1998), *After Our Likeness: The Church as the Image of the Trinity*, Grand Rapids: Eerdmans

Walker, A. (1996), *Telling the Story: Gospel Mission and Culture*, London: SPCK

Walker, A. (1998), *Restoring the Kingdom: The Radical Christianity of the House Church Movement*, Guildford: Eagle

Walls, A. (1996), *The Missionary Movement in Christian History: Studies in the Transmission of Faith*, Edinburgh: T & T Clark

Walser, R. (1993), *Running with the Devil: Power, Gender and Madness in Heavy Metal Music*, New England: Wesleyan University Press

Ward, G. (2005), *Cultural Transformation and Religious Practice*, Cambridge: Cambridge University Press

Ward, P. (1992), *Youth Culture and the Gospel*, London: Marshall Pickering

Ward, P. (1993), *Worship and Youth Culture*, London: Marshall Pickering

Ward, P. (1997), *Youthwork and the Mission of God*, London: SPCK

Ward, P. (2002), *Liquid Church*, Peabody: Henrickson/Carlisle: Paternoster

Ward, P. (2005), *Selling Worship* Carlisle: Paternoster

Ward, P. (2006), 'Mediating the Mediator: A Cultural Theology of Culture', in *Yale Institute for Sacred Music Colloquim: Music, Worship, Arts*, vol. 3, autumn

Ward, P. (2007), 'The Eucharist and the Turn to Culture', in Lynch, G. (ed.), *Between Sacred and Profane: Researching Religion and Popular Culture*, London: I. B. Tauris

Wenger, E. (1998), *Communities of Practice: Learning, Meaning, and Identity*, Cambridge: Cambridge University Press

Weston, P. (ed.) (2006), *Lesslie Newbigin Missionary Theologian: A Reader*, London: SPCK

Williams, R. (1958), *Culture and Society 1780–1950*, Harmondsworth: Penguin

Williams R. (1965), *The Long Revolution*, Harmondsworth: Penguin

Williams, R. (1976), *Keywords: A Vocabulary of Culture and Society*, Glasgow: Fontana

Williams, R. (1981), *Culture*, London: Fontana

Williams, R. (1994 [1961]), 'The Analysis of Culture', in Storey, J. (ed.), *Cultural Theory and Popular Culture: A Reader*, Hemel Hempstead: Harvester Wheatsheaf

Willis, P. (1977), *Common Culture*, Milton Keynes: Open University Press

Wuthnow, R. (1998), *After Heaven: Spirituality in America Since the 1950s*, Berkeley: California University Press

Zizioulas, J. (1985), *Being As Communion: Studies in Personhood and the Church*, Crestwood, NY: Saint Vladimir's Seminary Press

Websites

www.taize.fr/en_article3148.html, accessed 25 June 2007
www.vineyardusa.org/about/history.aspx, accessed 5 Feb. 2008
www2.hillsong.com/church/default.asp?pid=10, accessed 5 Feb. 2008
www.vineyardrecords.co.uk/ministry/index.html, accessed 5 Feb. 2008
http://secure.hillsong.com, accessed 29 Sept. 2006

Recording

Iris DeMent, *Lifeline*, Flariella Records FER–1004

Index of Names and Subjects